1 0 0 % B R U S S E L S

(m)

1 0 0 % B R U S S E L S

There's so much to experience in Brussels. Where to begin? Of course, you'll want to meet Manneke Pis, climb the Atomium, and finally see where the European Union gathers. But also be sure to stroll through the many wonderful shopping malls, experience nostalgia at the comics museum, sit at a sidewalk café on the Grote Markt, and enjoy a delicious meal at a good restaurant. Visit the theater in the evening, or go dancing at a trendy nightclub. This guide will take you by everything you want to see in no time at all: sightseeing, shopping, culinary delights, and adventure. The easy-to-use maps will show you the way.

100% BRUSSELS: EXPLORE THE CITY IN NO TIME!

Contents

HOTELS   7

TRANSPORT   14

GRAND PLACE AND LOWER BRUSSELS   16

SABLON AND MAROLLES   36

PLACE ROYALE AND BOTANIQUE   56

THE EU QUARTER AND SHOPPING ON ANSPACH   76

IXELLES AND ST. GILLES   96

LAEKEN AND RUE BLAES   116

NIGHTLIFE   136

INDEX   140

100% Easy-to-Use

To make this guidebook easy-to-use, we've divided Brussels up into six neighborhoods and provided a detailed map for each of these areas. You can see where each of the neighborhoods lies in relation to the others on the general map in the front of the book. The letters Ⓐ to Ⓢ will also let you know where to find attractions in the suburbs, hotels, and nightclubs, all described in detail later on in the guidebook.

In the six chapters that follow, you'll find detailed descriptions of what there is to do in the neighborhood, what the area's main attractions are, and where you can enjoy good food and drink, go shopping, take a walk, or just be lazy. All addresses have a number ①, and you'll find these numbers on the map at the end of each neighborhood's chapter. You can see what sort of address the number is and also where you can find the description by looking at its color:

⚫	= sights	🔴	= shopping
⚪	= food & drink	🔵	= nice to do

6 WALKS

Every chapter also has its own walk, and the maps all have a line showing you the walking route. The walk is described on the page next to the map, and it will take you past all of the most interesting spots and best places to visit in the neighborhood. You won't miss a thing. Not only will you see the most important sights, museums, and parks, but also special little shops, good places to grab lunch, and fantastic restaurants for dinner. If you don't feel like sticking to the route, you'll be able to find your way around easily with the descriptions and detailed maps.

PRICE INDICATION FOR HOTELS AND RESTAURANTS

To give you an idea of hotel and restaurant prices, you'll find an indication next to the address. The hotel prices mentioned are - unless otherwise stated - per double room per night. The restaurant prices are - unless otherwise stated - an indication of the average price of a main course.

NATIONAL HOLIDAYS

Next to the general holidays Good Friday, Easter, Whitsun, and Ascension Day, Belgium observes the following public holidays:

1 January	- New Year's Day
1 May	- Labour day
21 July	- Belgium National Day
15 August	- Assumption
1 november	- All Saints' Day
11 november	- Armistice Day
25 & 26 December	- Christmas

Note, that if any one of these fall on a Sunday, the next becomes a holiday.

DO YOU HAVE A TIP FOR US?

We've tried to compile this guide with the utmost care. However, the selection of shops and restaurants can change quite frequently in Brussels. Should you no longer be able to find a certain address or have other comments or tips for us concerning this guide, please let us know. You'll find our address in the back of the book.

(A) CAFÉ MÉTROPOLE

Hotels

There are tons of hotels in Brussels, ranging in price from €54 at the quaint Hotel Welcome, to €409 at the upscale Conrad International on avenue Louise. All hotels are listed under the official five-star system, with one star signifying the fewest number of amenities and five stars representing the most. Don't be fooled, however, into thinking that five-star rooms are the best. Some of the coziest rooms are located in small hotels, which just happen not to boast a 24-hour concierge service or a fitness center. Here are a few of the nicest rooms in the heart of the city center.

High End

Ⓐ **The Métropole** is a well-known hotel in the city center. Built at the turn of the century, this magnificent retreat has maintained its spectacular belle époque style, with glistening chandeliers and marbled floors. The hotel also has a wellness center, a café and a fantastic French restaurant. A breakfast buffet is included in the price of your room.
31 place de brouckère, telephone 022 17 23 00, rates from €310 (€111 on weekends), metro de brouckère

Ⓑ **Amigo Hotel** is a remarkable 18th century-style hotel right near Grand Place. The building once served as a prison, but a miraculous renovation has turned it into one of the best five-star hotels in Brussels. It's perfect for honeymoons and romantic getaways. Service includes a multilingual staff, concierge services and valet parking. A continental breakfast (served in your room) is included in the price.
1-3 rue de l'amigo, telephone 025 47 47 47, rates from €321 (€148 on weekends), metro centrale

(c) Location! Location! Location! Step outside of Brussels' Central Station and **Le Meridien** seems to wait with arms open to rescue the weary traveler. This is a top-quality hotel boasting royalty among its clientele. Located minutes from Grand Place, its luxurious rooms are spacious, bright, comfortable and outfitted with all the high-tech options every business traveler needs. Also try the hotel's excellent restaurant, L'Epicerie, and cozy bar, Jermyn's Street.

3 carrefour de l'europe, telephone 025 48 42 11, rates from €347 (breakfast included), metro centrale

(D) **The Conrad International Brussels** opened in 1993 and is situated in the posh avenue Louise area, the heart of Brussels' upscale shopping district. Designer boutiques are lined up just outside the door of this retreat, which offers a full-service restaurant, cozy cocktail bar and well-equipped fitness center with an indoor swimming pool. Enjoy nearby sites such as the Palais de Justice and the Bois de la Cambre.

71 avenue louise, telephone 025 42 42 42, rates from €285 (breakfast included), metro louise

(E) **The Radisson SAS** is one of the most beautiful hotels in Brussels. The lobby features a gorgeous winter garden laid out around a sky-high ancient city wall dating from 1134. Choose from one of the 281 rooms available in four different styles: Scandinavian, Oriental, Italian and Royal Club. The hotel's restaurant, The Sea Grill, is one of Brussels' top-ten eateries.

47 rue du fosse-aux-loups, telephone 022 19 28 28, rates from €347 (breakfast included), metro centrale

(F) **Le Plaza** is a centrally located, five-star hotel built in 1930. In its heyday, it was much loved by celebrities, including Brigitte Bardot, Gary Cooper, Humphrey Bogart, Viviane Leigh and Clark Gable, just to name a few. The hotel closed in 1976, was completely refurbished and then re-opened in 1996 with much success. Enjoy dinner at the restaurant, L'Estérel, before turning in to your comfortable room equipped with all the necessary amenities, including a private fax and digital safe.

118-126 boulevard adolphe max, telephone 022 27 67 00, rates from €350, metro rogier

PARC DU CINQUANTENAIRE

BUILDING COUDENBERG

Mid-Range

Ⓖ **Le Dixseptième** is a charming hotel offering a welcome change from larger hotel chains. Housed in a beautifully restored 17th century mansion, it offers rooms named after Belgian painters. Each room boasts a different décor, most are equipped with antique furnishings and lovely wall hangings and a few even come with fireplaces. The breakfast buffet, which is included in the price, offers a variety of breads and cereals, plus hot options like eggs and sausages.
25 rue de la madeleine, telephone 025 02 57 44, rates from €176, metro centrale

Ⓗ The four-star **Alfa Louise** hotel, built in 1994, is conveniently located near the fine shops and offices of avenue Louise. All rooms are spacious and comfortable, and have a balcony and private bathroom. In the evening, relax to the soothing sounds of live jazz in the Jazz Bar.
212 avenue louise, telephone 026 44 29 29, rates from €161, metro louise

Ⓘ The large **Bedford Hotel** is extremely well situated - just a stone's throw from Grand Place. Though recently renovated, it maintains its charm with the comforts of a large, modern four-star hotel. All rooms come equipped with their own bathroom and color TV providing a fine selection of in-house films. In the evening, enjoy the live piano entertainment in the lounge. If you're traveling by car, you're in luck. This is one of the few hotels in the city center with a large parking garage.
135 rue du midi, telephone 025 07 00 00, rates from €145 (promotional week rate) or €81 (promotional weekend rate), metro de brouckère

Lower-Range

Ⓙ **Hotel Welcome**, just a ten-minute walk from Grand Place, is the smallest hotel in Brussels. Each of its ten rooms has been renovated and includes modern comforts such as private bathrooms with shower or bath, radios and hair dryers (an amenity not always found in European hotels). The fine seafood restaurant, La Truite d'Argent, is on the ground floor.
5 rue de peuplier, telephone 022 19 95 46, rates from €54 (breakfast an additional €7.50), metro sainte catherine

(K) **Le Dôme** hotel is actually made up of two buildings, Dome 1 and Dome 2, situated right next to each other. One was originally constructed in Art Deco style but, unfortunately, many of its original features have been lost over the years. Gustav Klimt reproductions are found in most rooms. The walk to the Grand Place area is a little over ten minutes, but the hotel is located very near the Jardin Botanique.

12/13 boulevard du jardin botanique, telephone 022 18 06 80, rates from €87 (breakfast included), metro rogier

(L) The beautiful **Hotel Ustel** is housed in a 19th century property that was completely renovated in 1992. Today, all rooms have their own bathroom, color TV, telephone and hair dryer. The hotel's bar, Les Fringues, has a large outdoor terrace lying between the hotel and the restaurant, La Grande Ecluse. This historic property is protected by the city because it was once the location of a major sluice, which was used to regulate the flow of the Zenne River in order to protect Brussels from flooding.

6-8 place de l'aviation, telephone 025 20 60 53, rates from €107, metro lemonnier

JANNEKEN PIS

Transport

There are several reliable public transportation options to get around Brussels. A public transport ticket costs €1.40, lasts for one hour and is valid on all buses, metros and trams. If you plan to use public transportation quite frequently, consider purchasing a Day Pass (carte d'un jour) for €3.60 or a five- (€6.20) or ten- (€9) journey ticket.

The **metro** consists of two lines - #1 and #2. Line #1 runs east to west through the center of the city and then divides into two (#1A and #1B) to service the suburbs. Gare Centrale train station is on this line. Line # 2 circles the city and runs through train stations Gare du Midi and Gare du Nord.

There is also a prémetro system, which essentially is a tramline running underground through the center of the city, operating from the St. Gilles area, through Gare du Midi, through Bourse in the center of Lower Town and on to Gare du Nord. The **tram** system is pretty vast and will take you just about anywhere you need to go in the town center as well as out to the suburbs, with stops located throughout Brussels.

STIB **buses** also operate everywhere and bus stops are easily recognizable. When you receive your ticket, you must have it stamped in a validation machine before you commence your journey. In the case of the metro, these machines are located in the stations before you reach the platform; on trams and buses, they are located by the door. Stamp your ticket each time you ride, including when you transfer from one vehicle to another. This is an honor system, but there are occasional random inspections. Don't get caught empty-handed!

To take a **taxi**, you must line up at one of the various taxi stands located around the city. The stands are at all train stations, at most upscale hotels and also at Bourse, Porte de Namur and De Brouckère. Rates start at €2.35, plus €1 per km. Taxis can also be ordered by phone by calling Taxis Orange at 023 49 43 43 or Taxis Verts at 023 49 49 49.

Grand Place and Lower Brussels

Welcome to the crossroads of Brussels. Here, in the heart of the city, visitors can sample each of Belgium's treasures, whether it's a taste of chocolate, a refreshing beer, a scrumptious waffle or insight into the birth of the comic strip. Grand Place, the exquisite square that dominates the area, is by far one of the most (if not the most) magnificent squares in Europe. Filled with tourists and locals enjoying a drink on a terrace or purchasing flowers at the

1

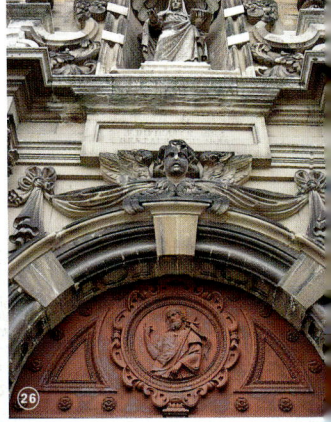

market, the atmosphere is absolutely electric. Elsewhere in this neighborhood, you'll find the core of Belgium's financial exchange, a fashionable shopping street and some of the best bars in town. When visiting Brussels, make this district your first stop!

6 Musts!

Mokafé

Enjoy a traditional breakfast at Mokafé and browse a newspaper.

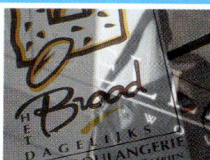

Antoine Dansaert

Go shopping in Antoine Dansaert.

Centre Belge de la Bande Dessinée

Go to Centre Belge de la Bande Dessinée and learn about the country's comic history.

Café Métropole

Stop for tea at the stylish Café Métropole.

Arenburg-Galeries

Arenburg-Galeries: while in a foreign land check out a foreign film.

L'Archiduc

Enjoy cocktails and live jazz at L'Archiduc.

● **Sights**
● **Shopping**
○ **Food & drink**
● **Nice to do**

Sights

⑥ **Janneken Pis** was commissioned in 1985 to be the female counterpart to Manneken Pis. Reached through a tangle of passages off the Rue des Bouchers, the statue squats mischievously over the Fountain of Loyalty.
impasse de la fidelité, metro gare centrale

⑧ **Grand Place** has been called the most splendid market square in Europe. Its esplanade is completely enclosed by tall, gabled, Flemish Renaissance buildings. Daily commerce and a colorful flower market liven up the square, and on Sundays there is a terrific bird market. It is even more splendid at night, in the golden glow of dramatic floodlights.
grand place, metro bourse or gare centrale

⑨ The **Musée de la Ville de Bruxelles** is housed in Maison du Roi, a gorgeous 16th century mansion on Grand Place. The museum, dedicated to the legacies of Brussels, follows the development of art, politics, economics and social life throughout the city's history. There is also a quirky display of more than 600 of Manneken Pis' costumes.
10 grand place, telephone 022 79 43 50, open apr-sep, tue-fri 10am-12.30pm & 1.30pm-5pm, sat-sun 10am-1pm, oct-mar, tue-fri 10am-12.30pm & 1.30pm-4pm, sat-sun 10am-1pm, admission €2.50, metro bourse or gare centrale

⑩ The **Musée du Cacao et du Chocolat** is appropriate in a country where the average inhabitant consumes 18 pounds of chocolate a year. Watch demonstrations by a chocolate master from Tuesday to Friday (between 10am and 3pm) and sample different types before buying your favorites!
13 grand place, telephone 025 14 20 48, open tue-sun 10am-5pm, admission €5, metro bourse or gare centrale

⑪ In the basement of the Brewer's House on Grand Place, you'll discover the **Musée de la Brasserie**, a small but comprehensive exhibition detailing the evolution of beer brewing. This is also the headquarters of the CBB, the Confederation of Belgian Brewers.

13 grand place, telephone 025 11 49 87, open daily 10am-5pm, admission €3, metro bourse or gare centrale

⑫ **Hôtel de Ville**, or Brussels' Town Hall, is the focal point of Grand Place. The wings of this grand structure, built in the 15th century, are united by a Gothic tower rising 318 feet and crowned by a statue of St. Michael. Inside is a host of rooms housing art from the 17th and 18th centuries.

grand place, telephone 022 79 64 71, open mon-thu 10am-12.30pm & 1.30pm-5pm, sat-sun 10am-1pm, metro bourse or gare centrale

(13) In the tiny arcade under 8 Grand Place, is a small golden statue of **Evrard t' Serclaes**. Legend has it that rubbing the wrist of this statue of a 14th century Belgian hero will bring good luck and grant long forgotten wishes.
8 grand place, rue charles buls, metro bourse or gare centrale

(14) Emotionally, **Manneken Pis** is to Brussels what the Eiffel Tower is to Paris and the Statue of Liberty is to New York. Cast in bronze in 1619, this tiny nude statue has been attacked, destroyed and recast repeatedly throughout its history. Today, locals dress the naughty garçon in a variety of costumes: one day a musketeer, the next Elvis!
corner of rue de l'étuve, metro bourse

(15) **Notre Dame de Bon Secours** is a 17th century church designed by Willem de Bruyn, architect of the Maison des Brasseurs on Grand Place. This is another delightful example of Flemish Renaissance architecture. Services are held on Sundays at 11am.
rue du marché au charbon, telephone 025 14 91 13, open daily 9am-5pm, metro anneessens or bourse

(16) **Notre Dame aux Riches Claires** is a uniquely charming building. Built in 1665, presumably by a pupil of Rubens, it is completely asymmetrical. Services are held at 10am on Sundays.
21 rue des riches claires, telephone 025 11 09 37 for visiting hours, metro bourse

(26) For a fantastic example of Flemish baroque, visit **St. Jean Baptiste au Béguinage**. Founded in the 13th century, the church - with its magnificent honey-hued façade - was once the center of Brussels' largest béguinage, or abbey. Services are held at 5pm on Saturdays, and at 10am and 8pm on Sundays.
place du béguinage, telephone 022 17 87 42, open tue 10am-5pm, wed-fri 9am-5pm, 1st, 3rd & 5th sat of every month 10am-5pm, sun 9.30am-noon, metro sainte-catherine

(27) Architect Léon Suys designed the **Bourse**, or stock exchange, in 1873. Its classic style is adorned by a myriad of sculptures depicting sea and domestic trade, representing the building's primary function - financial trading. Guided tours of the building are available.
boulevard anspach, telephone 025 09 12 11, admission free, metro bourse

(28) The **Scientastic Museum** is a great stop for science buffs. Designed to bring the world of science alive for children, playful adults will enjoy it as well. Exhibits range from optical illusions to defying gravity.
level 1 metro bourse, telephone 027 32 13 36, open mon-fri 12.30pm-2pm, sat-sun and school holidays 2pm-5.30pm, admission €4.40, metro bourse

(29) **St. Nicolas** is the oldest church in Brussels and is named after the patron saint of merchants. Founded in the 11th century, the church is a model of medieval construction, with a dark and haunting interior. Services are at 8am, 11.30am and 5pm on Sundays, with English language services at 10am and 6.30pm.
1 rue au beurre, telephone 025 13 80 22, open mon-fri 7.30am-6.30pm, sat-sun 9am-6pm, metro bourse or de brouckère

(34) **Notre Dame du Finistère** is a light and elegant church located in the midst of a chaotic shopping street. Most of the church's construction took place during the 18th century, and its baroque interior is truly magnificent. Services take place at 9.15am, 12.10am and 5pm daily.
rue neuve, telephone 022 17 52 52, open mon-sat 8am-5.45pm, sun 8am-noon, metro de brouckère or rogier

(35) The **Centre Belge de la Bande Dessinée** (The Belgian Center for Comic Strips) is situated in a stunning Art Nouveau warehouse built in 1903 by Victor Horta. A captivating permanent exhibition features comics from more than 650 artists. Check out Slumberland, the fantastic shop. The largest library of comic strips in the world and a delightful café will round a visit off.
20 rue des sables, telephone 022 19 19 80, open tue-sun 10am-6pm, admission €6.20, metro botanique, de brouckère or rogier

⑤ RUE DES BOUCHERS

Food & drink

(4) **Mokafé** is a great place for coffee and pastry, or for a full lunch of croque monsieurs, pasta or a variety of sandwiches. This place is quite popular with locals, and is always crowded and smoky. A prime spot for people watching!
9 galerie de roi, telephone 025 11 78 70, open daily 8am-midnight, metro gare centrale

(5) **Rue des Bouchers** is a small passageway in the shadow of Grand Place. This gastronomic street is a tourist trap, however it is quite interesting to pass through. The restaurant doors are always open, with waiters trying to lure customers, and at the first sight of sun, chairs and tables line the alley. If you must eat here, consider Aux Armes de Bruxelles or the Belgian chain Chez Léon for moules-frites.
rue des bouchers, metro gare centrale

(17) The hip and happening **Zebra Bar** is operated by the owners of Bonsoir Clara and Kasbah. Its sprawling sidewalk café is fantastic on a warm day, and the wide variety of food (pastas and sandwiches) and beers is quite tasty. By night, the place is hopping, filled with trendsetters.
33 place st. géry, telephone 025 11 09 01, open daily noon-2am, metro bourse

(18) **Le Java** is noisy, crowded and loads of fun. Located near several bars and restaurants, this is a great place to begin or end an evening. Check out the bar's surface - encrusted with bottle tops!
14 rue st. géry, telephone 025 12 37 16, open daily 5pm 5am, metro bourse

(20) **L'Archiduc** is the quintessential Brussels nightspot. Ring to open the door and you'll find yourself in what looks like the setting of an old Fred Astaire film. Sundays at 5pm, there is live jazz, and on Saturdays is 'Jazz After Shopping', which can be enjoyed for free.
6 rue antoine dansaert, telephone 025 12 06 52, open daily 4pm-late, admission €7.50, drinks €5, metro bourse

㉑ **Kasbah** doesn't stop hopping. The ambiance is lively, the décor inviting and the crowd attractive. Choose from starters such as taboule or eggplant salad before moving on to authentic couscous dishes with meat or chicken, as well as vegetarian couscous. Save room for dessert and mint tea.
20 rue antoine dansaert, telephone 025 20 40 26, open mon-fri noon-2.30pm & 7pm-11pm, sat 7pm-11pm, price €16, metro bourse

㉒ **Bonsoir Clara** is a delightful restaurant with a young, convivial and trendy atmosphere. The cosmopolitan menu includes French, Italian and Asian cuisine. The ambiance is incredibly cozy, the food delicious, the staff friendly and the wine selection divine.
22-26 rue antoine dansaert, telephone 025 02 09 90, open mon-thu noon-2.30pm & 7pm-11pm, fri-sat noon-2.30pm & 7pm-midnight, price €25, metro bourse

㉕ For generations, fishermen sailed into the **Place St. Catherine** selling their fresh catch at the Vismêt (fish market). Today, this neighborhood boasts several seafood restaurants, like Jacques (inexpensive and traditional), François (top class) and Medussa (contemporary charm).
place st. catherine, metro sainte-catherine

㉜ **Café Métropole** is part of the five-star Hôtel Métropole. Like the hotel, it is sophisticated, elegant and dripping in charm. Stop off here for a flute of champagne and a nibble on a tasty pastry.
31 place de brouckère, telephone 022 19 23 84, open mon-thu 9am-1am, fri-sat 9am-2am, metro de brouckère

Shopping

(1) **Galeries Saint-Hubert**, Europe's first indoor shopping mall, is over 200 years old and holds a large variety of upscale boutiques (Lacoste, Longchamp, etc.), several cafés, a movie theatre, bookstores and small offices. In 1837, King Leopold I instructed the young architect Jean-Pierre Cluysenaars to turn rue Saint-Hubert into an arcade. The result, divided into the King's, Queen's and Princes' Galeries, is one of the world's most beautiful arcades.
rue du marché aux herbes, open 24 hours a day, metro gare centrale

(3) The middle of the magnificent Galeries Saint-Hubert is the perfect setting for **Delvaux**, a high-end boutique selling handbags and accessories. Since its inception in 1829, Delvaux has been the Belgian name for handmade leather handbags. While it is most popular with a mature clientele, its younger and more affordable line, Deux, ensures that the bags are found on the arms of most stylish ladies.
31 galerie de la reine, telephone 025 12 71 98, open mon-sat 10am-6.30pm, metro gare centrale

(19) **Rue Antoine Dansaert** is the hippest shopping street/neighborhood in Brussels. It has a bohemian feel and is filled with home design studios, hip designer clothing boutiques and a smattering of art galleries. This is where fashion's elite hangs out!
rue antoine dansaert, metro bourse

(23) **Stijl Men/Women**, located on the popular rue Dansaert, is the mecca of contemporary Belgian haute couture. This boutique features designs from alumni of Antwerp's renowned Fashion Academy, and includes a fabulous selection of styles from Ann Demeulemeester, Dries van Noten, Martin Margiela, Dirk Bikkembergs and many others.
74 rue antoine dansaert, telephone 025 12 03 13, open mon-sat 10am-6.30pm, metro bourse

㉔ **Via della Spiga** is named after the famous fashion street in Milan. Pass through this stylish boutique's narrow hallway and enter its spacious showroom loaded with threads from top designers such as Vivian Westwood, Yves St. Laurent, Wim Neels, Masaki Matsishina, Paul Smith and Alexander McQueen.

42 rue antoine dansaert, telephone 025 02 20 97, open mon-sat 10.30am-6.30pm, metro bourse

㉛ **Sterling Books** serves up English literature right in the heart of Brussels. This fantastic bookstore stocks a large variety of fiction and non-fiction, as well as a dizzying selection of English language magazines. All items are priced in pounds sterling, but are kindly converted into euros for you by the friendly staff.

38 rue du fossé aux loups, telephone 022 23 62 23, open mon-sat 10am-7pm, sun noon-6.30pm, metro de brouckère

�33 Hold on to your bags as you try to navigate through **rue Neuve**. This crowded pedestrian shopping street houses virtually every clothing chain ever created. It's absolutely packed on the weekends, but if you must get your H&M, Etam and Mexx, then this is the place to be.

rue neuve, metro de brouckère

STIJL

Helmut Lang (10m^2)
Dries Van Noten (13m^2)
Ann Demeulemeester (12m^2)
Martin Margiela (11m^2)
A.F. Vandevorst (7m^2)
Olivier Theyskens (5m^2)
Jurgi Persoons (3m^2)
Xavier Delcour (4m^2)

Encore (Xm^2)
Angelo Figus (4m^2)

Nice to do

(2) **Arenburg-Galeries** is an extraordinary movie theater comprising two halls and seating 427 people. Both theaters are air-conditioned - which is a rare treat in Belgium! Enjoy celebrated international art films and shorts, most shown in their original format with subtitles in French and Dutch.
26 galerie de la reine, telephone 025 12 80 63, open daily 1pm-10.30pm, metro gare centrale

(7) **Théâtre de Toone** has been in the Toone family for seven generations. It is world-renowned for its marionette performances of great theatrical works such as Cyrano de Bergerac and Hamlet. Though the performances are mostly conducted in Bruxellois (a mix of Flemish and French), the experience more than makes up for the language barrier.
21 petite rue des bouchers, telephone 025 11 71 37, open daily noon-midnight, metro de brouckère

(30) **Théâtre de la Monnaie** is a spectacular theatre at the forefront of opera and is considered one of the most exciting opera houses in the world.
place de la monnaie, 4 rue leopold, telephone 022 29 12 00, box office open tue-sat 11am-6pm, metro de brouckère

EDON

LE SINGE un film de AKTAN ABDYKALYKOV

LE SINGE un film de AKTAN ABDYKALYKOV

un casting à vous couper le souffle, à vous de le

scénario et réalisation
Jean-Luc

Grand Place and Lower Brussels

The tour begins in the magnificent Galeries St. Hubert (1) (3) (2) (4). Head down rue de Bouchers (5), adjacent to the Galeries on the left (if you're coming from the mall's entrance on Marché aux Herbes). Make a tiny detour to see Janneken Pis (6) in a tiny alley off to the right of Bouchers. Next, purchase tickets for an afternoon show at Théâtre de Toone (7) on Petite rue des Bouchers. Cross over rue du Marché aux Herbes and continue until you reach the stunning Grand Place (8) (9) (10) (11) (12) (13). Out of Grand Place, follow rue Charles Buls (later rue de l'Etuve) until you reach the corner of rue du Chêne. Here find Manneken Pis (14), the infamous peeing statue. Continue northeast on rue des Grandes Carmes and turn right on rue du Midi. A quick left on rue du Lombard and another on rue du Marché au Charbon will lead to Notre Dame du Bon Secours (15). Back on rue du Marché au Charbon, a left on rue des Riches Claires leads to Notre Dame aux Riches Claires (16). Follow the side street, rue St. Géry, to place St. Géry and stop off for a drink or lunch (17) (18). Then walk north on pont de la Carpe and turn left (or right) on Antoine Dansaert (19) (20) (21) (22) (23) (24) and get ready to shop. Marché aux Grains (a right off of Dansaert) leads to place St. Catherine and the Vismét (25). From there, a left on quai au Bois à Brûler and an immediate right on rue de Peuplier leads to St. Jean Baptiste au Béguinage (26). Now head south on rue de Béguinage on to rue de la Vierge Noire, going still further south on P. Deveaux until you reach the Bourse (27) in front of you and the Scientastic Museum (28) to your right. Rue de la Bourse runs along the north side of the Bourse and will take you straight to St. Nicolas (29). A left on rue de Fripiers leads to Théâtre de la Monnaie (30). From here, a minor detour turning right on rue du Fossé aux Loups leads to Sterling Books (31) and the opposite direction down the same street leads first to Rue Neuve (33) (34) to the right, or further down to blvd. Adolphe Max Laan where you can stop at Café Métropole (32) for afternoon tea or coffee. Returning to rue Neuve, a right on rue aux Choux, another right on rue du Marais and an immediate left on rue de Sables leads to the Centre Belge de la Bande Dessinée (35).

6 Musts!

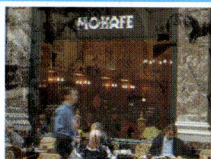

Place du Jeu de Balle

Sift through the flea market at Place du Jeu de Balle.

Le Pain Quotidien

Breakfast doesn't get any more Belgian than at Le Pain Quotidien.

Place du Grand Sablon

Explore, shop and browse the windows at Place du Grand Sablon.

Eglise Notre Dame du Sablon

Discover Eglise Notre Dame du Sablon, where the wealthy once worshipped.

Blvd. Waterloo and Av. de la Toison D'or

Stroll down Blvd. Waterloo and Av. de la Toison D'or, Brussels' 'Fifth Avenue'.

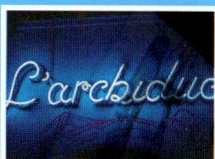

Atelier de la Truffe Noire

Atelier de la Truffe Noire specializes in dishes made from truffles.

⬤ Sights
⬤ Shopping
⬤ Food & drink
⬤ Nice to do

more workers. Today, the dichotomy between the two neighborhoods still exists, with Sablon teeming with antique shops, posh restaurants and step-gabled houses, and the Marolles filled with dingy dives, a daily flea market and overcrowded tenements. The two distinct atmospheres are both equally charming.

1. Galeries St. Hubert
2. Arenburg-Galeries
3. Delvaux
4. Mokafé
5. rue des Bouchers
6. Janneken Pis
7. Théâtre de Toone
8. Grand Place
9. Musée de la Ville de Bruxelles
10. Musée du Cacao et du Chocolat
11. Musée de la Brasserie
12. Hotel de Ville
13. Statue Evrard t' Serclaes
14. Manneken Pis
15. Notre Dame de Bon Secours
16. Notre Dame aux Riches Claires
17. Zebra Bar
18. Le Java
19. Antoine Dansaert
20. L'Archiduc
21. Kasbah
22. Bonsoir Clara
23. Stijl Men/Women
24. Via della Spiga
25. Place St. Catherine
26. St. Jean Baptiste au Béguinage
27. Bourse
28. Scientastic
29. St. Nicolas
30. Théâtre de la Monnaie
31. Sterling Books
32. Café Métropole
33. rue Neuve
34. Notre Dame du Finistère
35. Centre Belge de la Bande Dessinée

Sablon and Marolles

The Sablon neighborhood historically served as the artisan's quarter, the powerhouse of the textile trade in Brussels. Meanwhile, at the southern end of the city, the Marolles district was developing, with a host of carpenters, builders and prostitutes taking up residence there. The poorer people in Marolles attended church at Notre Dame de la Chapelle, while the more sophisticated Sablon residents attended Notre Dame du Sablon. As the Sablon area increased in wealth, the Marolles neighborhood filled up with

St. Catherine

De Broockère

Continue Tour 4

Bourse

Bruxelles

Grand Place

Manneken Pis

St. Nicolas

Théâtre Royal de la Monnaie

Cath. St. Michel

Centre Belge de la Bande Desinée

Finish

Start

Finish Tour 4

Gare Centrale

Parc

Tour Noire

Terre-Neuve

Parc D Bruxelles

Street names (selection):
Rue De Flandre, Quai Aux Briques, Quai Au Bois À Brûler, Rue Du Chien Marin, Rue Du Rouleau, Rue Du Béguinage, Grand Hospice, Rue Du Marronnier, Rue De Laeken, Rue Vander Elst, R. Des Hirondelles, Rue Du Cirque, Rue Aux Fleurs, Boulevard En, Nieuwbrugstr., Boulevard Adon, R. De La Fiancée, R. De La Fiancée, Rue Neuve, Pont Neuf, Finistère, Rue Aux Choux, La Blanchisserie, Rue Des Cendr, Rue Du Damier, Rue Du Canon, Rue Des, La Blanchisserie, Rue Saint-Michel, Rue Aux Choux, Rue Du Marais, Rue Du Persil, R. Des Sables, Rue Du Melboor, Rue Saint-Laur, Rue Antoine Dansaert, Rue Sainte-Catherine, Rue Melsens, Rue De La Vierge Noire, Place Du Samedi, Rue Des Augustins, Place De Brouckere, Pl. De Brouckere, Passage Du Nord, Impasse Du Cheval, Rue Du Fossé Aux Loups, Rue D'argent, R. D'argent, R. Des Boiteux, Rue Du Marais, Rue Des Comédiens, R. Des Comédiens, R. Des Poissonniers, Rue Des Halles, Boulevard Anspach, Rue Grétry, L'évêque, Rue Des Fripiers, Rue De L'ecuyer, R. Des Princes, Rue De Ligne, Rue Saint-Laur, Blvd. Pach., Rue De La Banque, De Berlaimont, Rue De, Rue Paul Devaux, Rue Auguste Orts, Rue Jules Van Praet, Rue Henri Maus, Rue De La Bourse, R. De La Bourse, Agora, Rue Petit, Au Beurre, Rue Au Beurre, Rue Des Bouchers, Petite Rue Des Bouchers, Galerie Du Roi, R. Des Dominicains, R. Montagne Aux Herbes Potagères, R. D'assaut, R. D'arenberg, Rue De L'impératrice, Rue Du Loxum, Rue Du Marché, Rue Du Marquis, R. Des Paroissiens, R. Des Colonies, Rue Des Colonies, Rue De Ligne, Rue De Chancellerie, Borgval, Rue Saint-Géry, Rue Des Claires, Rue De L'eclipse, Rue Plattesteen, Impasse Du Midi Madrille, Rue Du Charbon, Rue Du Marché Au Charbon, R. Du Marché Au, Rue De Grands Carmes, Rue De La Goutière, R. Des Moineau, Rue Des, Rue De L'étuve, Rue Des Pierres, Rue De L'amigo, R. Chair Et Pain, Pl. R. Et Pain, Rue De L'étuve, Marché Aux Herbes, Galerie De La Reine, Galerie Agora, Rue Des Éperonniers, Rue De La Madeleine, Galerie Bortier, R. De L'hôpital, Rue Saint-Jean, Rue Des Chapeliers, Rue De La Violette, Rue De Lombard, Rue Des Alexiens, Rue Des Poinç, Rue Des Villers, R. De La Collège, R. De La Montagne, Rue Cardinal Mercier, Rue Du Bois Sauvage, Pl. Sainte-Gudule, Treurenber, Putterie, Rue Du Cantersteen, Rue Terarken, Mont Des Arts, Boulevard De L'impératrice, Place De L'albertine, Pl. De L'albertine, Boulevard De L'impératrice, Rue Ravenstein, Galerie Ravenstein, Place De La Nation, Pl. De La Nation, La R. Montagne, Du Parc, Pl. Royale

Numbered markers: 1, 2, 3, 4, 5, 6, 7, 8-13, 14, 15, 16, 17, 18, 19, 20-22, 23, 24, 25, 26, 27, 28, 29, 30, 31, 32, 33, 34, 35

Sights

(1) **Tour d'Angle**, or 'Corner Tower', is a remnant of Brussels' first set of city walls. At one time, it was connected to the Tour de Villiers and the Tour Noire, whose ruins can also be found within the city. Two centuries after the construction of the first city walls, a second, more formidable, set was erected.
boulevard de l'empereur, metro gare centrale

(3) The **Eglise des Brigittines**, an Italo-Flemish church built in the 1660s, has served as a prison, a poorhouse, a dance hall and a butchery in addition to being home to the order that founded the church, named after St. Brigitte, a Swedish mystic and saint.
1 rue des visitandines, telephone 025 06 43 00, open only for concerts, metro gare centrale

(4) **Eglise Notre Dame de la Chapelle**, founded in 1134, is where renowned Belgian artist Pieter Bruegel the Elder married, and is the home of a small memorial site dedicated to him. In the chapel are several interesting works of art, including a unique 16th century wooden statue and elegant stained-glass windows. Services are held on Sundays at 8.00am, 9.30am, 10.30am, 4.30pm and 6.30pm.
place de la chapelle, telephone 025 12 07 37, open jun-sep daily 9am-4pm, oct-may daily noon-4pm, metro gare centrale or anneessens

(7) The **Fountain of Minerve**, which adorns Sablon square, was a gift from the Earl of Ayelsbury as a token of gratitude to the city of Brussels for granting him asylum during his exile from England.
place du grand sablon, metro gare centrale

(10) The **Musée des Postes et Telecommunications** is a fascinating place to figure out the 'method to the madness' behind postal systems. You'll discover that by 1500, the Turn and Taxis family, who hailed from Italy, were operating the most effective and expansive post and communications system in Europe. Today the museum houses a complete collection of Belgian stamps and telecommunications equipment.
40 place du grand sablon, telephone 025 11 77 40, open tue-sat 10am-4.30pm, admission free, metro gare centrale

⑫ **Eglise Notre Dame du Sablon** lies between the Sablon and the Petite Sablon areas. Brussels' wealthiest citizens once patronized this stunning Gothic church, which features marvelous stained-glass windows in its interior.

38 rue de régence, telephone 025 11 57 41, open mon-fri 9am-5pm, sat 9.30am-5pm, sun 1pm-5pm, metro porte de namur

⑬ The park in the center of the **Place du Petit Sablon** was designed in 1890. The Art Nouveau railings are divided into 48 columns, each capped by a statuette representing the ancient guilds of Brussels.

metro porte de namur

⑭ Construction on **Palais d'Egmont** began in the 16th century, and enlargements were made later in the 1900s. Once home to 16th century Count Egmont, today the palace is used as a reception hall for the Minister of Foreign Affairs. Other past residents include Louis XV and Voltaire.

8 petit sablon, telephone 025 13 89 40, not open for public, metro louise

⑮ The Palace may not be open to the public, but the **Jardin d'Egmont** (gardens) are. Enjoy a stroll through the gardens, but try to disregard the Hilton Hotel looming ominously in the background.

boulevard waterloo, telephone 025 13 89 40, open sunrise-sunset, metro louise

⑯ On the corner of Place Poelaert is the **British War Memorial**, a tribute from the British people to the Belgians, who assisted British soldiers and prisoners during World War I.

place poelaert, metro louise

26 In an effort to turn Brussels into one of the most impressive capitals in the world, King Leopold the II instructed one of his favorite architects, Joseph Poelaert, to build the imposing **Palais de Justice**. Constructed from 1866-1883, it was for a long time the world's largest building.
place poelaert, telephone 025 08 65 78, open mon-fri 9am-3pm, admission free, metro louise

29 **Eglise de Minimes**, built between 1700 and 1715, is a simple yet elegant church founded by the Minimes, an order of monks. During the French occupation of 1796, the site was closed and used as a place to store artillery. The church was restored in 1819 and is today famous for hosting classical music concerts.
62 rue des minimes, telephone 025 11 93 84, open daily 10am-1pm, metro louise

30 The **House of Pieter Bruegel the Elder** is a charming red brick, step-gabled house from the 16th century. Bruegel is thought to have lived here from 1563 until his death in 1569.
132 rue haute, open to groups with written request, metro louise

35 **Musée de l'Hôpital Sainte-Pierre** is the location of the Centre Public d'Aide Sociale de Bruxelles. The hospital was originally founded in the 12th century to treat leprosy, and as that disease disappeared in Europe, was maintained through various gifts from wealthy donors. A collection of 17th century furniture, tapestries and other treasures is on display throughout the building.
298a rue haute, telephone 025 43 60 55, open wed 2pm-5pm, admission free, metro porte de hal

36 The **Musée du Folklore** is a branch of the Royal Museums of Art and History. It displays carnival traditions and old toys and games spanning the Middle Ages to modern day.
porte de hal, boulevard du midi, telephone 025 34 15 18, open tue-sun 10am-5pm, admission €4, metro porte de hal

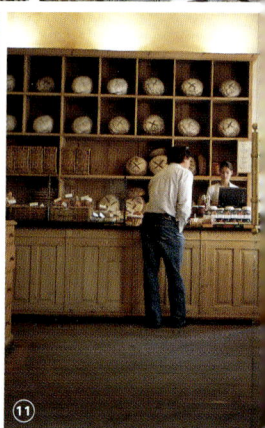

Food & drink

(2) **Comme Chez Soi** is the best restaurant in Brussels - hands down. Chef Pierre Wynants is a mastermind, conjuring the most delicious Franco-Belgian dishes. Despite its off-the-beaten-track location, the restaurant has earned three Michelin stars and offers diners an intimate Art Nouveau setting in which to enjoy their meal. Make a reservation ahead of time; this place is always fully booked.
23 place rouppe, telephone 025 12 29 21, open tue-sat noon-1.30pm & 7pm-9.15pm, price for four-course lunch €50, dinner €99, metro anneessens

(8) **Wittamer** is perhaps the most celebrated cake and candy shop in Brussels. From croissants to rich chocolate, this is a place that cannot be missed. With lines of people waiting outside the door, there's no denying its popularity!
6-12 place du grand sablon, telephone 025 12 37 42, open mon 10am-6pm, tue-sat 7am-7pm, sun 7am-6pm, metro louise

(9) When the weather is warm and dry, **La Kartchma**'s pleasant sidewalk café is filled with classy Belgians sipping wine and sampling a wide variety of beers. It's a great place to visit at any time.
17 place du grand sablon, telephone 025 12 43 10, open daily 10am-4am, price €10, metro louise

(11) **Le Pain Quotidien**, which can also be found in Paris and New York, started right here in Belgium. This place serves up arguably the best 'oven fresh' bread in the city. The 'Daily Bread' is not only a bakery, but also a patisserie, deli, snack bar and coffee house. Be sure to try the selection of open sandwiches!
11 rue des sablons, telephone 025 13 51 54, open mon-fri 7.30am-7pm, sat-sun 8am-7pm, price €8, metro louise

㉕ **Atelier de la Truffe Noire** serves up everything from foie gras to sandwiches, but as its name suggests, truffles are the specialty of the house. Chef Luigi Cicieriello opened the atelier as a less expensive alternative to his more upscale La Truffe Noire. The minimalist décor is truly inviting, as is the wondrous selection of pastries. There is also a breakfast menu from 8.30am-11am.

300 avenue louise, telephone 026 40 54 55, open mon-sat 8.30am-6.30pm, price €20, metro louise

㉗ **Café Le Perroquet** is a delightful Art Nouveau-style café frequented by the stylish people who fill the Sablon area. The simple lunch selection (salads and pita sandwiches) is listed on the blackboard.

31 rue watteeu, telephone 025 12 99 22, open daily 10.30am-1am (food served noon-1am), price lunch €7, metro louise

㉛ At **Indigo**, you can buy brocante (a fancy word for 'junk') as well as sandwiches. The avocado, Roquefort and bacon salad is delicious, and the desserts are also yummy!

160 rue blaes, telephone 025 11 38 97, open tue-fri 10am-3pm, sat-sun 9.30am-4pm, price €6, metro porte de hal

㉞ **De Skieven Architek** means 'crooked architect', a derogatory name given to Joseph Poelaert who tore down part of the Marolles neighborhood to build the ostentatious Palais de Justice. Located on the edge of the daily flea market, this is a great place to enjoy a beer or a coffee. The breakfast is pretty decent too!

50 place du jeu de balle, telephone 025 14 43 69, open daily 6am-1am, price €10, metro porte de hal

Shopping

(5) **Place du Grand Sablon** is the gorgeous setting for a fantastic weekend antique market. As befits the area and the surrounding shops, folks who know their Louis XIV from their Louis XV peddle a dazzling variety of collectibles here. Make sure to pass by Pierre Marcolini at no. 39 to sample some delicious Belgian chocolates.
place du grand sablon, flea market open sat 9am-6pm, sun 9am-2pm, metro gare centrale or louise

(6) **Emporio Armani** is the answer for dapper dressers who crave Giorgio's designer look. Watch the tanned bodies sporting designer sunshades pass through its doors, and catch a whiff of heavy cologne wafting in the air.
37 place du grand sablon, telephone 025 51 04 04, open mon, wed-sat 11am-6pm, sun 11am-6pm, metro gare centrale or louise

(17) **Boulevard Waterloo** and **Avenue de la Toison D'or** make up the upscale shopping district of Brussels. They are to this city what Fifth Avenue is to New York. Chanel, Hermes, Louis Vuitton and Cartier are all here. Get your credit card ready for action!
boulevard waterloo and avenue de la toison d'or, metro louise

(18) **Gucci** beckons from the corner, its five seductive letters gleaming in silver. If you want a bargain, walk on by. But if you are slave to Tom Ford's amazingly sexy designs, then step right up.
66 boulevard waterloo, telephone 025 11 11 82, open mon-sat 10am-6pm, metro louise

(19) The **Chanel** boutique is small and exclusive, just as it should be. A wonderful selection of dresses and suits awaits the sophisticated lady. Don't forget to enquire about the stunning jewelry collection.
63 boulevard waterloo, telephone 025 11 20 59, open mon-sat 10am-6pm, metro louise

(20) **Ralph Lauren** is just the place for those who crave the classic American look. From housewares to suits, this shop provides everything you need for the Lauren leisure lifestyle.
52 boulevard waterloo, telephone 025 51 08 51, open mon-sat 10am-6pm, metro louise

(21) **Versace**'s clothes practically accost you as you walk by the window. Steamy and sexy, donning Donetella's designs are only for the daring.
64 boulevard waterloo, telephone 025 11 85 59, open mon 1pm-7pm, tue-sat 10am-12.30pm 1.30pm-7pm, metro louise

(22) **Avenue Louise** is an extension of the exclusive shopping area found on Waterloo and Toison d'Or. Down this stretch are slightly less expensive stores like Zara for men and women, located across the street from each other.
avenue louise, metro louise

(23) Need a new watch? **Cartier** might have what you need - providing you've got the cash to spend! If you've got the funds, they've got the time…
1 avenue louise, telephone 025 37 51 61, open mon-sat 10am-6pm, metro louise

(24) **Thierry Mugler** offers up contemporary, sleek designs. For the super style-conscious, this store is an absolute must. Don't worry if the sales people seem less than friendly… they're just jealous!
80 avenue louise, telephone 025 02 64 22, open mon-sat 10am-6.30am, metro louise

(28) **Verscheuren** is the center for Belgian lace. Watch a lace-maker practice her craft, view a video on the history of lace production, and while you're at it, purchase a few pieces to take back home for mom!
16 rue watteeu, telephone 025 11 04 44, open daily 9am-6pm, metro louise

(32) An old firehouse, **Caserne des Pompiers**, across from the flea market, is the setting for a variety of businesses. Check inside for several junk shops, an art gallery, a couple of bookstores and a café.
rue blaes, metro porte de hal

(33) The **Place du Jeu de Balle's Flea Market** is the gathering place for a motley crew of street peddlers and antiques vendors. Arrive early to get the best deals and the choicest of selections.
place du jeu de balle, flea market open daily 7am-2pm, metro porte de hal

Sablon and Marolles

Begin the tour at the Corner Tower ① on the south side of Boulevard de l'Empereur. From here, continue west and turn right on to rue d'Accolay. Cross rue de l'Etuve and turn left on place Rouppe ②. Continue west on Avenue de Stalingrad and make the second left on rue van der Weyden. Turn left on rue des Visitandines ③ and follow to place de la Chapelle ④. Make a right on rue Rollebeek and continue through the Grand Sablon area ⑤ ⑥ ⑦ ⑧ ⑨ ⑩ ⑪. Turn left on rue de Régence ⑫ and then turn right into the Petite Sablon ⑬. Make a left on rue aux Laines ⑭ ⑮, and a right turn on rue des Quatres Bras will lead you to Place Poelaert ⑯. Rue des Quatres Bras in the opposite direction leads directly to the intersection of boulevard Waterloo/avenue de la Toison d'Or ⑰ ⑱ ⑲ ⑳ ㉑ and Avenue Louise ㉒ ㉓ ㉔ ㉕. After your shopping spree, return to Place Poelaert ㉖ and continue right on rue E. Allard. Turn left on rue Watteeu ㉗ ㉘ and again on rue des Minimes ㉙. Follow rue de la Porte Rouge on your right to rue Haute and turn left ㉚. Make another right on rue du Miroir and a left on the antiques and brocante shopping street rue Blaes ㉛ ㉜ until you reach place du Jeu Balle ㉝ ㉞. A left on rue de la Rasiere leads to rue Haute ㉟. Turn right and follow to Porte de Hal ㊱.

6 Musts!

Musée des Instruments de Musique

Start the day breakfasting on the fantastic terrace of Musée des Instruments de Musique Restaurant.

Musée d'Art Ancien

Browse Bruegels and explore Ensors at Musée d'Art Ancien.

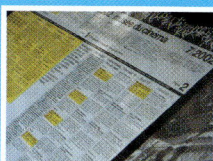

Musée du Cinema

Choose an art film or a silent film at Musée du Cinema.

Musée de la Dynastie

At Musée de la Dynastie, see how the royals lived.

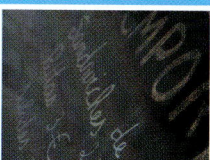

La Table de Merlin

La Table de Merlin is a small café and everything is 100% bio-friendly.

Mary Chocolatier

Don't leave this city without chocolates from Mary Chocolatier.

○ Sights
○ Shopping
○ Food & drink
○ Nice to do

3

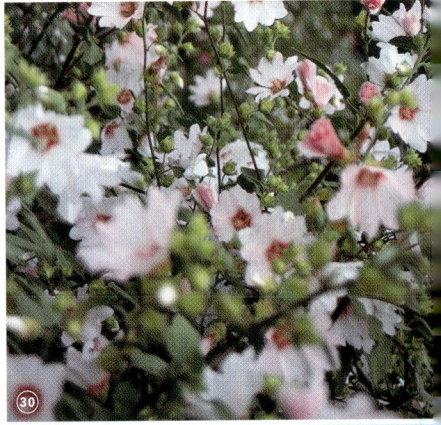

several mansions that have been transformed into museums. The quaint Royal Park sprawling across the center of this area is characteristic of this not-to-be-missed section of Brussels; sleepy yet charming.

1. Tour d'Angle
2. Comme Chez Soi
3. Eglise des Brigittines
4. Eglise Notre Dame de la Chapelle
5. place du Grand Sablon
6. Emporio Armani
7. Fountain of Minerve
8. Wittamer
9. La Kartchma
10. Musee des Postes et Telecommunications
11. Le Pain Quotidien
12. Eglise Notre Dame du Sablon
13. place du Petit Sablon
14. Palais d'Egmont
15. Jardin d'Egmont
16. British War Memorial
17. blvd. Waterloo and ave de la Toison D'or
18. Gucci
19. Chanel
20. Ralph Lauren
21. Versace
22. avenue Louise
23. Cartier
24. Thierry Mugler
25. Atelier de la Truffe Noire
26. Palais de Justice
27. Café Le Perroquet
28. Verscheuren
29. Eglise de Minimes
30. House of Pieter Bruegel the Elder
31. Indigo
32. Caserne des Pompiers
33. place du Jeu de Balle
34. De Skieven Architect
35. Musee de l'Hopital St.Pierre
36. Musée du Folklore

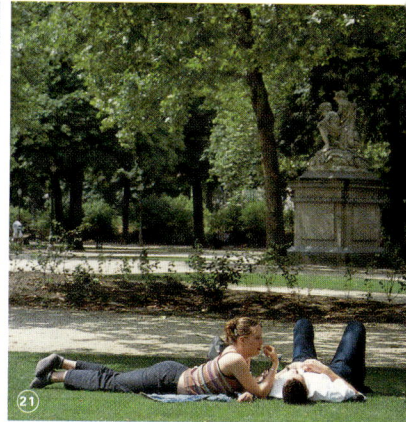

Place Royale and Botanique

Brussels is divided into Lower Town - the area around Grand Place - and Upper Town, whose entrance is marked by climbing the stairs of the Mont des Arts. Once at the threshold of Upper Brussels, you'll find yourself in the midst of several of Belgium's national treasures including the national library and art collection. As the aristocracy and the ruling classes once dominated this area, you shouldn't be surprised to stumble upon the Royal Palace and

Legend

- ⬤ Sights
- ⬤ Food & drink
- ⬤ Shopping
- ⬤ Nice to do

START

FINISH TOUR 6

CONTINUE TOUR 6

FINISH

Area labels

CENTRAL • Putterie
ANNEESSENS
LEMONNIER
BRUXELLES KAPELLEKERK
PORTE DE NAMUR
LOUISE
HÔTEL DES MONNAIES
PORTE DE HAL
PARVIS DE SAINT-GILLES
CONTINUE TOUR 6

Points of interest

Manneken Pis
Palais du Midi
Palais de Beaux-Arts
Palais Royal
Palais d'Egmont
Pa D Brux
Cité Fontainas
Terre-Neuve

MONT DES ARTS ①

Sights

(1) **Mont des Arts**, or 'Arts Hill', connects Upper Town (Place Royale) and Lower Town (Grand Place). In the mid-1950s, the area was restructured with the arrival of the Congress Center and the Royal Library Albert I. Enjoy a splendid view of Lower Town from the French terrace garden.
mont des arts, telephone 025 11 34 33, open daily 24 hours, admission free, metro gare centrale or parc

(2) Better known as Albertina, **Bibliothèque Royale Albert I** houses nearly 4 million books. As Belgium's national library, it contains a collection that began in the 15th century with copies of manuscripts from the Dukes of Burgundy. Since then, just about everything that has been published in Belgium has been included.
4 boulevard de l'empereur, telephone 025 19 53 56, open mon-fri 2pm-5pm, sat 9am-6pm, admission free, metro gare centrale or parc

(3) The **Musée de l'Imprimerie** (Museum of Printing) contains old printing presses of several varieties including enormous hand-pulled presses. If you're interested in the history of printing before Quark Express, this is a interesting stop.
bibliotheque royale albert I, 4 boulevard de l'empereur, telephone 025 19 53 56, open mon-sat 9am-5pm, admission €2.50, metro gare centrale or parc

(4) **Musée de Livre**, or the Book Museum, is a treasure to visit. One small, temperature-controlled room contains rare books that are over 1,000 years old. The earliest book printed in Europe (dating back to 1474) is also on display.
bibliotheque royale albert I, 4 boulevard de l'empereur,
telephone 025 19 53 57, open mon, wed, sat 2pm-5pm, admission €2.50, metro gare centrale or parc

(5) **Chapelle de Nassau** was once part of Hôtel de Nassau, which, during the 16th century, belonged to the politically influential Nassau family. The chapel is now the location for temporary exhibitions related to books and the written word.
bibliotheque royale albert I, 4 boulevard de l'empereur, open daily 10am-4.50pm, admission €2.50, metro gare centrale or parc

(7) In the splendid Art Nouveau-style Old England house (created by renowned architect Saintenoy) is the **Musée des Instruments de Musique**. With a collection 7,000 strong and 1,500 instruments on display, this is the largest museum of its kind in the world. Visitors can hear the sound of each instrument via a set of headphones and stop in at the museum's shop or library.

2 rue montagne de la cœur, telephone 025 45 01 30, open tue-wed, fri 9.30am-5pm, thu 9.30am-8pm, sat-sun 10am-5pm, admission €5, metro gare centrale or parc

(9) **Place Royale** is a magnificently symmetrical square offering a panoramic view over Lower Town. Restoration of the façades of the buildings facing the square has rejuvenated the area, making this a picturesque locale amid the bustling city traffic.

place royal, metro parc

(10) The **Statue of Godfrey de Bouillon** was erected in the center of Place Royale in 1848 by King Leopold I. De Bouillon was a legendary hero who, after having fought in the Crusades, was asked to be King of Jerusalem. He refused, preferring instead to be entitled 'Defender of the Holy Sepulcher'.

place royale, metro parc

(11) The **Eglise Saint-Jacques-sur-Coudenberg** church was erected in 1775 to resemble a Roman temple. It once served as the royal chapel and was a 'temple of law' during the French Revolution.

1 impasse borgendael, place royale, telephone 025 11 78 36 or 025 02 18 25, open daily 10am-5.45pm, admission free, metro parc

(12) The **Musée d'Art Ancien**'s collection, which spans the 15th to 18th centuries, primarily focuses on classic works from artists from the Low Countries - Hans Memling, Pieter Bruegel the Elder, Pieter Paul Rubens, etc.

3 rue de la régence, telephone 025 08 32 11, open tue-sun 10am-5pm, admission €5, metro gare centrale or parc

(13) The **Musée d'Art Moderne** is connected to the Musée d'Art Ancien by an underground passageway. It features the work of Belgian surrealists like Magritte, as well as works from Picasso, Dali, Matisse, Warhol and others.
3 rue de la régence, telephone 025 08 32 11, open tue-sun 10am-1pm & 2pm-5pm, admission €5, metro gare centrale or parc

(14) **Chapelle Royale** was built in 1760 by Charles of Lorraine. It is a real gem to see if you can get inside (opening hours are sporadic) as its neoclassical sanctuary is flooded with light. It became a Protestant Church in 1804 and in 1831, became the chapel of King Leopold I.
2 place du musée, telephone 025 13 23 25, opening hours vary, admission free, metro gare centrale or parc

(15) The **Service de Chalcographie** holds an exhibit of engraving plates and is part of the National Library. Over 5,400 plates are displayed here, including old views of the city and images of abstract art.
1 place du musée, telephone 025 19 56 31, open mon-fri 9am-12.45pm, 2pm-4.45pm, admission free, metro gare centrale or parc

(16) **Palais Royale** is the Belgian king's official residence. When he is in, a flag is flown to mark his presence. The rather austere building dates back to the 19th century, and its cold grandeur helps to explain why the royal family chooses to have their daily residence in the parks of Laeken. A changing of the guard (nothing as grand as that in England) occurs each day at 2.30pm.
place des palais, telephone 025 51 20 20, staterooms open late july to early september 10.30am-4.30pm, admission free, metro parc

(17) **Musée de la Dynastie** is a royal exhibition found in the House of Bellevue, which used to be an 18th century hotel for wealthy travelers. Located adjacent to the Royal Palace, this grand building displays a rich collection of memorabilia from the Belgian Royal Dynasty.
7 place des palais, telephone 025 11 55 78, open tue-sun 10am-4pm, admission €6.50, metro gare centrale or parc

(18) **Palais des Beaux Arts** was designed by Art Nouveau architect Victor Horta and constructed in 1928. It was the first building in the world to house concert halls, a theatre, exhibition spaces, shops, a cinema and a restaurant all under the same roof.

23 rue ravenstein, telephone 025 07 84 68, open tue-thu, sat-sun 10am-6pm, fri 10am-8pm, admission around €7.50 (varies with exhibition), metro gare centrale or parc

(20) **Musée du Cinéma** houses two theaters, one showing art films each evening at 6.15pm (often in their original language), and one screening silent films accompanied by live piano music at 7pm and 9pm every night. There are exhibits demonstrating early experimental film techniques and portraying the history of film as well.

palais des beaux-arts, 9 rue baron horta, telephone 025 07 83 70, open daily 5.30pm-10.30pm, admission free, film €2.25, metro gare centrale or parc

(21) The 18th century **Parc de Bruxelles** is a central highlight marking Brussels' Upper Town. Filled with elegant fountains and statues, this park was once a popular commons for Brussels' wealthy elite to take afternoon strolls. Today, Eurocrats use it for jogs on their lunch hour.

rue royale, metro parc

(22) **Palais de la Nation** is an imposing neoclassical building that is part of Belgium's government quarter. Since 1831, the two 'arms' of government (Chamber of Representatives of the People and the Senate) have been meeting in the National Palace, built in 1779 when Maria-Theresia of Austria acceded to the throne.

1 & 2 place de la nation rue de la loi, telephone 025 49 81 36, open mon-sat 10am, 11am, 2pm & 3pm for groups only (must book at least 2 months ahead), admission free, metro parc

㉔ **Musée de l'Hotel Charlier** is a turn-of-the-century house filled with tapestries, period furnishings, silverware and a collection of art by the likes of James Ensor and the original proprietor himself, Guillaume Charlier, an artist well known in Brussels in the early 1900s.
16 avenue des arts, telephone 022 18 53 82, open mon 10am-5pm, tue-wed 1.30pm-5pm, thu-fri 1.30pm-4.30pm, admission €2.50, metro arts/loi or madou

㉗ **Cathédrale des Sts Michel et Gudule** is the location for Belgium's royal weddings and funerals. Construction began in the 13th century and took over 200 years to complete. During the 16th and 17th centuries, several chapels were added. Concerts featuring religious or classical music are regularly held here.
place ste gudule, telephone 022 17 83 45, open mon-fri 8am-6pm, sat-sun 8.30am-6pm metro gare centrale or parc

㉘ **Colonne du Congres** was designed in 1850 by architect Joseph Poelaert, who later built the Palais de Justice. An image of Leopold I, Belgium's first king, rests atop the 47-meter-high column, which was erected in commemoration of the National Congress that established the Belgian constitution in 1831. The eternal flame at the base is in remembrance of victims of the two World Wars.
rue royale, metro parc or botanique

㉚ **Jardin Botanique** is the location of a marvelous glasshouse built for the Brussels Horticultural Society in 1826. Today it is the home of the Centre Culturel de la Communauté Française Wallonie-Bruxelles, the cultural center for the Walloon (French-speaking) community.
236 rue royale, open daily 11am-6pm, admission free, metro botanique

㉝ **Eglise Sainte Marie** is a wonderful 19th-century church well worth visiting. Best described as neo-Byzantine, it is capped by a copper dome and has rose-tinted windows. Within its octagonal shape are several semi-circular chapels.
rue royale, telephone 022 45 45 77, open mon-fri 11am-1pm, sat-sun 3pm-5pm, metro botanique

Food & drink

(8) The **Musée des Instruments de Musique Restaurant** is perched on the top floor of the Old England Building and offers one of the best views of Lower Brussels. While the food isn't overwhelmingly ingenious, dining on the terrace more than makes up for it. Classic dishes - pastas, salads, soups and sandwiches - are available.
2 rue montagne de la cœur, 6th floor, telephone 025 02 95 08, open tue-wed, fri-sun 9.30am-4.30pm, thu 9.30am-9.30pm, price €8, metro gare centrale or parc

(25) **La Table de Merlin** is a totally environment-friendly restaurant serving up a variety of dishes, both meat and vegetarian. Enjoy dining in this cozy little establishment that only seats 22 people.
53 rue de la croix de fer, telephone 025 02 00 08, open mon-fri 9am-5pm, price €10, metro madou or parc

(32) **De Ultieme Hallucinatie** is one of the most interesting places in Brussels. Housed in an authentic Art Nouveau mansion, it contains a winter garden and its own grotto, a brasserie and a gourmet restaurant serving fish and wild game. The restaurant's name comes from Art Nouveau designer Victor Horta's habit of dining on hallucinogenic mushrooms.
316 rue royale, telephone 022 17 06 14, open mon-fri 11am-2pm, sat 4pm-2am, price brasserie €15, restaurant €30, metro botanique

MUSÉE DES INSTRUMENTS DE MUSIQUE RESTAURANT ⑧

Shopping

(6) **Librarie Histoire** is a fantastic French-language bookshop peddling a variety of art and history books as well as general interest books and a selection of CDs. The quaint two-story shop is a pleasure to browse through.
76 coudenberg, telephone 025 13 99 90, open mon-sat 9am-6pm, metro gare centrale

(26) **Le Grand** should satisfy your sweet tooth as you roam the streets of Brussels. Choose from a selection of pastries like apple tarts and éclairs, a host of chocolates - from pralines to Snickers - and delicious cookies.
45 rue da la croix de fer, telephone 025 11 34 16, open daily 6.30am-6.30pm, metro madou or parc

(29) **Mary Chocolatier** is the official chocolate source for the Belgian Royal family. The pictures of the King and Queen gracing the cash register show the two royals sporting terrifically wide grins. They must have just tasted a crunchy praline-filled chocolate morsel.
73 rue royale, telephone 022 17 45 00, open mon-sat 9.30am-6pm, metro parc or botanique

Nice to do

⑲ **Théâtre du Rideau de Bruxelles** is a francophone theatre company founded in 1943. The company is well known for its intriguing contemporary theatre productions. It produced the first French performance of Tennessee Williams' A Streetcar Named Desire, and guess what…they even offer babysitting services!
23 rue ravenstein, telephone 025 07 83 60, metro gare centrale

㉓ The **Théâtre Royal du Parc** is an 18th century theatre that can only be visited on a guided tour with a group. Otherwise, one has to be satisfied with the model sitting in the foyer. Classic and modern French plays are performed here.
3 rue de la loi, telephone 025 05 30 30, metro parc

㉛ **Le Botanique** is situated inside the conservatory of the Parc du Jardin du Botanique. The 'artistic space' includes an art gallery, two theatres and a small cinema. It's a great venue to catch a contemporary theatre performance or a live concert.
236 rue royale, telephone 022 26 12 11, admission €7.50 - €15, metro botanique

THÉÂTRE ROYAL DU PARC (23)

Place Royale and Botanique

To begin your discovery of Belgium's national treasures, first mount the steps at Mont des Arts ① and climb the stone steps to the right of the center garden to reach the Albertina ② ③ ④ ⑤. Continue up the stairs at the top of the garden until you reach Coudenberg. Cross the street and continue up rue Mont de la Cour ⑥ ⑦ ⑧. At the top find Place Royale ⑨ ⑩ ⑪. A right on rue de la Regence will take you to the national art museums ⑫ ⑬ and as you exit the museums turn left down a small cobbled street called rue de Musée which leads to Place de Musée ⑭ ⑮. Return to Place Royale and continue straight on Rue Royale. Immediately turn right on Place des Palais ⑯ ⑰. Again return to rue Royale and turn left on rue Baron Horta and again left on rue Ravenstein ⑱ ⑲ ⑳. Return once more to rue Baron Horta and cross over rue Royale for entrance into Parc Royale ㉑. At the northern end of the park on rue de la Loi is the Palais de la Nation ㉒. Turn right down rue de la Loi ㉓ and cross rue Ducale and boulevard du Regence. Here turn left on avenue des Arts ㉔. Continue down the avenue until you reach Madou metro. Turn left and walk down rue de la Croix de Fer ㉕ ㉖, cross over rue Royal and follow rue Treurenberg until you reach the St. Michel and Gudule Cathedral ㉗. Follow rue de Ligne north until you reach Place du Congrès ㉘ ㉙. Continue heading north on rue Royale for the final stops ㉚ ㉛ ㉜ ㉝.

6 Musts!

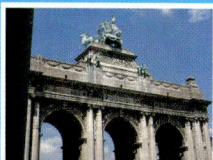

Parc du Cinquantenaire

Unpack a breakfast of warm breads at Parc du Cinquantenaire.

Maison Paul de Cauchie

Visit Maison Paul de Cauchie for amazing Art Nouveau.

Info Point Europe

Learn everything about the European Union at Info Point Europe.

Musées Royaux d'Art et d'Histoire

Visit Musées Royaux d'Art et d'Histoire (Musée du Cinquantenaire).

European Parliament

Visit the European Parliament Buildings.

Musée Wiertz

Discover the works of a man who was both gifted and disturbed at Musée Wiertz.

○ **Sights**
○ **Shopping**

○ **Food & drink**
○ **Nice to do**

is a welcome oasis in the midst of the rather stale government buildings, and offers a host of fantastic museums. A metro ride takes you from the EU district to Boulevard Anspach, a thoroughfare built over the former river Senne, which once ran through the city. A variety of small shops, the slightly garish Anspach shopping mall and other storefronts compete for your attention here.

1. Mont des Arts
2. Bibliothèque Royale Albert I
3. Musée de l'Imprimerie
4. Musée de Livre
5. Chapelle de Nassau
6. Librairie Histoire
7. Musée des Instruments de Musique
8. Musée des Instruments de Musique Restaurant
9. Place Royale
10. Statue of Godfrey de Bouillon
11. Eglise St-Jacques-sur Coudenberg
12. Musée d'Art Ancien
13. Musée d'Art Moderne
14. Chapelle Royale
15. Service de Chalcographie
16. Palais Royale
17. Musée de la Dynastie
18. Palais des Beaux Arts
19. Théâtre du Rideau de Bruxelles
20. Musée du Cinéma
21. Parc de Bruxelles
22. Palais de la Nation
23. Théâtre Royal du Parc
24. Musée de l'Hotel Charlier
25. La Table de Merlin
26. Le Grand
27. Cathédrale des Sts Michel et Gudule
28. Colonne du Congres
29. Mary Chocolatier
30. Jardin Botanique - Centre Culturel de la Communauté Française Wallonie-Bruxelles
31. Le Botanique
32. De Ultieme Hallucinatie
33. Eglise Sainte Marie

The EU Quarter and shopping on Anspach

13

9

Brussels is not only the capital of Belgium, it's also the capital of Europe. Its central location and the multilingual capabilities of its inhabitants are only some of the reasons why the city's designation as the 'heart of Europe' is so fitting. Brussels is filled with diplomats (Eurocrats), and the quarter situated around Parc Léopold is the area where most of the EU buildings are located. Because of the '9-to-5' atmosphere, most shops here close early, the place is deserted on the weekends and area bars cater to young foreign interns looking to unwind after a day with the 'suits'. Parc Cinquantaire, however,

START

FINISH

BOTANIQUE

BRUXELLES CONGRES

DE BROUCKERE

BRUXELLES CENTRAAL

MADOU

ART-LOI

PARC

Parc De Bruxelles

Centre Belge de la Bande Desinée

Théâtre Royal de la Monnaie

Cath. St. Michel

Théâtre du Parc

Palais de Beaux-Arts

Palais Royal

N.D. du Sablon

LES

Rue Des Hirondelles

Pl. De Brouckere

Pl. De Broeckere

Impasse Du Cheval

R. Du Fossé Aux Loups

R. Neuve

Rue Saint-Michel

Rue Aux Choux

R. Aux Choux

R. Du Canol

R. Du Dan

R. Du Marais

R. De L'ommegang

Rue Des Sables

R. Du Meiboom

Jardin Botanique

AV. GALILÉE

Galilée

Rue Galilée

Av. Brialmont

Rue RC

La Comète

Rue Tiber

Rue Traversière

Boulevard Pachéco

Blvd. Pachéco

Rue Schoffsheim

Av. Van Schoffsheim

Rue Van Orley

Rue De L'union

Rue Potagère

Quetelet

R. Du Persil

Rue Des Comédiens

Rue Saint-Laurent

Rue De Berlaimont

Rue Royale

Rue Vesale

Rue De Congrès

Pl. Du Congrès

Rue Du Gouvernement Provisoire

Rue Du Congrès

L'association

Rue Du Nord

Rue Des Cultes

Av. De L'astronomie

Rue Saint-Alph

Rue De Bériot

RUE SCAILQUIN

R. Saxe-Cobourg

L'alliance

Princes Léopold

R. Des D'argent Boiteux

Rue De La Banque

Rue De L'oratoire

Montagne De

R. De La Ligne

R. Du Moniteur

L'enseignement

Rue De La Presse

Rue Du Parlement

CHAUSSÉE DE LOUVA

Av. Des Arts

Rue De Louvain

Rue Hydraulique

R. Du Vallon

Rue Marie-Thérèse

Galerie Agora

R. Du Bois Sauvage

R. Des Paroissiens

Rue Des Colonies

Pl. De Louvain

Rue De Louvain

Rue Henri Beyaert

Rue De La Charité

Rue Du Marteau

Treurenberg

Putterie

Pl. Albertine

Mont Des Arts

Terarken Sols

R. Baron Horta

Rue Ravenstein

R. Montagne Du Parc

Place De La Nation

Pl. De La Nation

Rue De La Loi

Boulevard Du Régent

R. DE LA LOI

RUE DE LA LOI

Avenue Des Arts

Rue Joseph II

Rue Deux

Rue Royale

Villa Hermosa

Rue Du Musée

R. De La Paille

R. Du Paradis

Rue Sainte-Anne

R. De Ruysbroeck

Place Des Palais

Place De La Nation

Rue Ducale

Rue Zinner

Parc De Bruxelles

R. Lambermont

Rue Bodenbroek

R. De Régence

Petits Carmes

Rue Brederode

Pl. Du Trône

BLVD. DU RÉGEN

AVENUE DES ARTS

Guimard

Rue Commerce

Frère-Orba

Jacques

Montoyer

RUE BELLIA

Sights

Food & drink

Shopping

Nice to do

1
2-5
6
7
8
9-11
12-13
14-15
16-17
18
19
20
21
22
23
24
25
26
27
28
29
30
31
32
33

MUSÉE DE L'INSTITUTE ROYAL DES SCIENCES NATURELLES ⑦

Sights

(1) The **Palais des Académies** was constructed in 1823-1826 for the King of the Netherlands, William of Orange, while Belgium was under Dutch rule. Belgium gained independence soon thereafter. Today, it is the home of the francophone Royal Academy of Belgium, a group of notables from the scholarly world of the arts and sciences.
1 rue ducale, telephone 025 50 23 23, open only to groups with written request, metro trône

(2) The **Statue of Léopold II** standing in the place du Trône commemorates Belgium's second king, known for his acquisition of what was eventually renamed the Belgian Congo. The king had no male heirs (he had three daughters instead) so passed the crown on to his nephew, Albert I. He did eventually produce two other children, but they were by his mistress, 17-year-old Blanche-Caroline Delecroix, la Baronne de Vaughan.
place du trône, metro trône

(3) In the midst of towering, bland office buildings, find **square de Meeûs**, an attractive green 'island' filled with sculpture. Enjoy shaded respite under one of the nearby overhanging trees.
square de meeûs, metro trône

(4) **Place du Luxembourg**, lined with numerous cafés and restaurants, is a hub of activity during lunch hour. This is a favorite dining location for the many Eurocrats working at the nearby EU Parliament Buildings. The rail station, Gare du Quartier Léopold, was established in the mid-1800s. Exit it on the opposite side to reach the European Parliament.
place de luxembourg, metro trône

(7) The **Musée de l'Institute Royal des Sciences Naturelles** has perhaps the most impressive collection of dinosaurs in the world. Using a technique called 'dinamation', dinosaurs 'come to life' with blinking eyes, chomping mouths, and wagging tails. There are also exhibitions featuring mammals, fowl, invertebrates, sea life and an array of minerals, and an insect department filled with 5,000 creepy crawlies.

29 rue vautier, telephone 026 27 42 38, open tue-fri 9.30am-4.45pm, sat-sun 10am-6pm, admission €4, metro trône

(8) The paintings of Belgian Antoine Wiertz (1806-1865), who painted enormous works often depicting religious and mythical scenes, are preserved in the **Musée Wiertz**. Wiertz's themes are rather grisly - people being impaled or stabbed, and are titled appropriately: Thoughts and Visions of a Decapitated Head, Le Suicide and so forth.

62 rue vautier, telephone 026 48 17 18, open tue-fri 10am-noon & 1pm-5pm, every 2nd sat-sun 10am-noon & 1pm-5pm, admission free, metro trône

(9) The **European Parliament Buildings** opened in 1998 and are those shiny blue-green buildings peeping through the trees of Parc Léopold. Though technically the Parliament is based in Strasbourg, it meets three weeks out of every four in this building in Brussels. The 567 members of the body are elected officials.

rue wiertz, telephone 022 84 21 11, audio visits mon-thu 10am & 5pm, fri 10am, admission free, metro trône

(10) **Parc Léopold** runs behind the EU Parliament buildings and is the location for several institutions, including the Institute Solvay, the early Art Nouveau-styled Lycée Emile Jacqmain and the Institut Dentaire (dental school), built in 1935. Though this may not be the type of park in which you'll want to spend an afternoon relaxing (Parc Cinquantenaire is better for that), it does offer a pleasant little stroll along its winding paths.

rue belliard, metro trône

(12) The **Council of the European Communities**, in the Justus Lipsius building, is a sprawling peach-colored building that opened in 1995. It houses the Council of Ministers, an EU body composed of ministers of EU States who meet to discuss EU policies. The Council was established to be the major decision-making body of the EU. The building, however, is bursting at the seams, as it was built to house 12 EU member states instead of the current 15.
175 rue de la loi, telephone 022 99 61 11, metro schuman

(13) **Info Point Europe** was created to disseminate information about the European Union. You can't miss the mass of blue EU flags marking its location.
242 rue de la loi, telephone 022 96 55 55, open mon-fri 9am-4pm, metro schuman

(14) The **Berlaymont Building** is an oddly-shaped, cross-like building that used to house the European Commission. In 1991 it was discovered that the building was filled with dangerous levels of asbestos, and it has been closed ever since for 'cleaning'. It was hoped that the Commission (now in buildings scattered throughout the city) will return 'home' by the end of 2002. The Commission is an independent body of the EU whose function it is to see that the EU functions correctly. They propose policies and oversee the execution of treaties.
200 rue de la loi, metro schuman

(16) You can't miss the **Maison Saint-Cyr**, Gustave Strauven's (1878-1919) townhouse built for painter Georges Saint-Cyr in 1903. Its spider-like balconies and curvaceous, bronzed ironworks on the façade are truly splendid. The house is quite extravagant considering that the cash-strapped architect was limited to relying chiefly on brick and iron. This is his most celebrated work - and he was just 20 years old when he designed it.
11 square ambiorix, telephone 025 13 89 40, not open for public, metro schuman

(17) Victor Horta built **Maison Van Eetvelde** from 1895-1897 for the minister of the Belgian Congo. The house incorporates a variety of materials from the Congo, including mosaics, onyx used in its paneling and ceilings made of mahogany. It is now owned by the gas company, and its interiors can only be visited during a tour with the Atelier de Recherche et d'Action Urbane (ARAU).
4 avenue palmerston, call 022 19 33 45 for details, metro schuman

(18) **Maison Deprez-Van de Velde** is opposite of the Maison Van Eetvelde and was also designed by Victor Horta. It was built around the same time as its neighbor, though its features are slightly more conservative.
3 avenue palmerston, telephone 023 80 17 81, not open for public, metro schuman

(19) The **square Marie-Louise** is a graceful tree-lined park in the midst of an otherwise concrete office area. Its loveliness is enhanced by the variety of beautiful listed houses scattered about it and the quaint duck pond dominating its center.
square marie-louise, metro schuman

(22) For the 50th anniversary of Belgian Independence in 1880, King Léopold the II commissioned the construction of **Parc du Cinquantenaire**. Today you can visit some of the museums in the park or rest on the lawn and gaze at the nearby solemn manor houses. The park comes to life each year on July 21, the occasion of National Day, when fireworks illuminate the sky.
entrance avenue de la joyeuse entrée, open daily 24 hour, admission free, metro mérode or schuman

(23) The **Pavillon Horta** is a neo-classical piece by Art Nouveau master Victor Horta. Inside, one would find a series of seductive reliefs by Jef Lambeaux entitled Les Passions Humaines. We say 'one would' because the pavilion is kept locked out of respect for the neighboring mosque. However, you can peep through one of the crevices and just make out a voluptuous breast or a tantalizing thigh, if you're so inclined.
parc du cinquantenaire, telephone 027 41 72 11, open only to groups with written request, metro mérode or schuman

PARC DU CINQUANTENAIRE ㉒

PAR NOUS
POUR NOUS

(28) **MAISON DE PAUL CAUCHIE**

㉔ The **Musée Royal de l'Armée et d'Histoire Militaire** (Royal Museum of the Army and Military History) will be a sure hit with military enthusiasts. Grenades, guns, swords, cannons and other arms fill the display cabinets. Learn about the Belgian Revolution and visit the gigantic hangar, which houses fighter planes from World Wars I and II.
3 parc du cinquantenaire, telephone 027 37 78 11, open tue-sun 9am-noon & 1pm-4.30pm, admission free, metro mérode or schuman

㉕ **Autoworld** is a museum, not surprisingly, about autos! This is one of the world's finest collections of automobiles, with stunning antique luxury cars ranging from Bentley to Benz. The exhibition traces the history of motor vehicles from their inception to the 1980s; not bad for a country that doesn't even have its own automobile industry.
11 parc du cinquantenaire, telephone 027 36 41 65, open apr-oct daily 10am-6pm, nov-mar daily 10am-5pm, admission €4.95, metro mérode or schuman

㉖ The enormous **Musées Royaux d'Art et d'Histoire** (Musée du Cinquantenaire) was once the largest in the world. Every artistic discipline (except painting) is represented here, and there is an impressive collection of ancient Egyptian, Islamic, Oriental, Greek and Roman art. European decorative art is also represented, including a beautiful exhibition of ceramic and glass. One area of the museum is ingeniously dedicated to the blind, offering the opportunity to explore art using hands and ears.
10 parc cinquantenaire, telephone 027 41 72 11, open tue-fri 9.30am-5pm, sat-sun 10am-5pm, admission €3.70, free first wed of the month after 1pm, metro mérode or schuman

㉘ The **Maison de Paul Cauchie** was once the home of Paul Cauchie, a painter and architect. It was built during the heyday of Art Nouveau in 1905 and employs a technique called sgraffitti, whereby plaster is laid over colorful paints and designs are then scratched into the plaster to reveal the colors below.
5 rue des francs, telephone 026 73 15 06, open 1st weekend of the month 11am-1pm & 2pm-6pm, and by appointment, admission €3.70, metro mérode

Food & drink

(5) **Le Pullman** bar is legendary if only because it's always open. You can only imagine the cast of sordid characters who wander in and out of this place; from businessmen to after-hours club hoppers, this bar caters to everyone. Stop in for a beer any time of day and be a part of it.
12 place du luxembourg, open daily 24 hours, price €7, metro trône

(6) **Noé** is, for the most part, a vegetarian restaurant that caters to hordes of animal-friendly Eurocrats during its busy lunch hours. There is no menu, but there is a plat du jour that is usually a pretty delicious buy.
24 rue de trèves, telephone 025 12 85 20, open mon-fri 11.30am-4.30pm, price €7, metro trône

(11) **Maison Antoine** is one of the most well known fritures (a shop for French fries) in Brussels. Having been around for about 50 years, it is noted for selling the best French fries in the city. Be warned – the lines are long at lunchtime!
place jourdan, no telephone, open daily 11.30am-2pm, price €2, metro schuman

(15) **Bodeguilla** is a great basement dive serving Spanish tapas. It's located in the underground level of the upscale Le Jardin d'Espagne restaurant (whose chef is the official cook for the Spanish ambassador to Belgium). Mingle and snack with members of Brussels' Spanish expat community who no doubt frequent this place because of its cheap and tasty home cooking.
65-67 rue archimède, telephone 027 36 34 49, open mon-sat 7pm-11pm, price €5, metro schuman

LE PULLMAN ⑤

(20) **The Wild Geese** is one of the most popular haunts for the EU crowd, especially on Thursdays. It's an Irish pub, so it has all the electricity of a good old Celtic watering hole, and the food is pretty palatable as well. Try a stuffed baked potato with a side salad, a great snack to accompany your pint.

2-4 ave livingstone, telephone 022 30 19 90, open sun-wed 11am-1am, thu 11am-2am, fri-sat 11am-3am, metro schuman or madou

(21) **Kitty O'Shea's** can get a bit unruly - especially when there's Irish soccer on the TV - but that's part of what makes this place so great. Aside from the delicious Irish dishes and the endless flow of Guinness, the lads and lasses who frequent this place make it one of the rowdiest romps in the area!

42 boulevard charlemagne, telephone 022 30 78 75, open daily noon-2am, metro schuman

(31) The Belgian deli **Au Suisse** serves up a variety of specialties such as maatjes (Dutch herring) and filet americain (raw ground beef - meant to be eaten as is). There are plenty of items to choose from, and you can dine-in at one of two long counters and sample some pastries with your coffee.

73-5 boulevard anspach, telephone 025 12 95 89, open mon, wed-fri 10am-8pm, tue 10am-7.30pm, sat 10am-7pm, sun 7pm-9pm, metro bourse

Shopping

(27) The **Atelier de Moulages** (Casting and Molding Workshop) dates back to the late 19th century when it was set up to house craftsmen who supplied molded copies of famous statues. The workshop still has about 4,000 molds, taken from some of the greatest art collections around the world. Be sure to visit the storeroom, where thousands of casts of busts, statues and masks are located.
parc du cinquantenaire, telephone 027 41 72 94, open mon-fri 9am-noon & 1.30pm-3.45pm, metro mérode or schuman

(29) **Cristallerie Anspach** has it all - Baccarat, Waterford, Lalique and even the Belgian brand Val St. Lambert. Not surprisingly, this is a favored stop for visiting honeymooners.
123 boulevard anspach, telephone 025 12 76 96, open mon-sat 9.30am-6.30pm, metro bourse

(30) **Brüsel** is a popular comic-book store stocking over 8,000 new editions and specializing in underground French issues. The shop is named after a Belgian comic strip of the same title that depicts the architectural destruction of Brussels in the 1960s. The shop occasionally holds exhibitions.
100 boulevard anspach, telephone 025 02 35 52, open mon-sat 10.30am-6.30pm, sun noon-6.30pm, metro bourse

(32) **100% Design** is based on an interesting concept: make it in plastic and consumers will come. All kinds of home design goodies are here, in every form of plastic imaginable. Should you need a lava lamp or an inflatable chair (with a mohair pillow) to put the finishing touches on your living room, well… you're in luck!
30 boulevard anspach, telephone 022 19 61 98, open mon noon-6.30pm, tue-sat 10am-6.30pm, metro de brouckère

(33) The **Virgin Megastore** is just like every other Virgin Megastore - several levels of music, music and more music. In addition to the hundreds of thousands of CDs, the store includes listening stands and a selection of games.
30 boulevard anspach, telephone 022 19 90 04, open mon-thu & sat 10am-7pm, fri 10am-8pm, sun noon-7pm, metro de brouckère

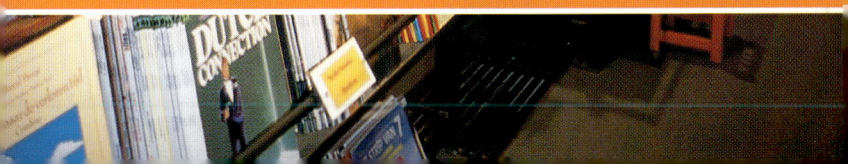

The EU Quarter and shopping on Anspach

WALKING TOUR 4 - THE EUROCRATS

Start at 1 rue Ducale ①, walk south to place du Trône ②. Continue on to rue du Luxembourg ③ until place du Luxembourg ④ ⑤. Once you've crossed the square, turn right on rue de Treves ⑥ and left on rue Godecharle until chaussée de Wavre, and turn left. Turn left on rue Wiertz, take the first right on rue Vautier ⑦ ⑧. Follow Vautier back out of the park on rue Wiertz to the European Parliament Buildings ⑨. Re-enter Parc Léopold ⑩ and follow a path, which eventually will lead to rue Belliard at the end of the park. Turn right on rue Belliard, turn right on chaussée d'Etterbeek until place Jourdan ⑪. Exit the square on rue Froissart and follow it north ⑫ to rond-point Schuman. Circle the rond-point along the right, cross rue de la Loi ⑭ (a detour on rue de la Loi will lead you to Info Point Europe ⑬), and turn right on rue Archimède ⑮ until square Ambiorix. Walk through the center of the square and find the Maison St-Cyr ⑯ on the corner. Turn left and continue around the square until avenue Palmerston, turn right on the avenue ⑰ ⑱. Palmerston; leads down to the square Marie-Louise ⑲. Walk counter-clockwise around the square until avenue Livingstone. Turn left on Livingstone ⑳ and continue until rue Stevin and turn right. For a 'beer break' turn left on boulevard Charlemagne ㉑. Otherwise, continue on rue Stevin until avenue de Cortenberg. Follow Cortenberg to the right until avenue de la Joyeuse Entrée, make a left and follow until the entrance to the Parc Cinquantenaire ㉒ at avenue J.F. Kennedy. Once in the park, the Horta Pavillon ㉓ is left, and the museums straight ahead down avenue J.F.K. ㉔ ㉕ ㉖. Just beyond the museums, turn left on avenue de la Chevalerie and right on avenue des Nerviens to the Atelier de Moulages ㉗. Retrace your steps and turn down avenue des Gaulois. Turn right on rue des Francs to the Maison de Cauchie ㉘ and a subsequent left on avenue des Celtes will take you to the Mérode metro station. If you're in the mood to do some shopping, take the metro to the Bourse prémetro stop, exit at boulevard Anspach ㉙ ㉚ ㉛ ㉜ ㉝ (look at map tour 1, page 35).

5

Like many trends, however, as quickly as the movement came, it petered out. Nonetheless, today some of the most beautiful Art Nouveau buildings have been left behind. Though most homes are not open to the public, Ixelles and St. Gilles are two fantastic Brussels neighborhoods, architecturally speaking, and a stroll through both should prove to provide a pleasant day.

6 Musts!

Hôtel Solvay

Delight in Art Nouveau architecture at Hôtel Solvay.

Musée Horta

aMusée Horta - designed and once inhabited by Victor Horta.

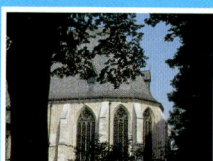

Bois de la Chambre

Have tea in the Bois de la Cambre.

Chaussée d'Ixelles

Spend money on the Chaussée d'Ixelles.

Matongé

Discover the Matongé neighborhood.

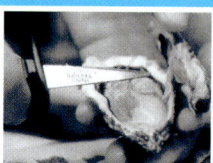

La Quincaillerie

Dine on oysters in trendy La Quincaillerie.

● **Sights**
● **Shopping**
○ **Food & drink**
● **Nice to do**

1. Palais des Acadamies
2. Statue of Léopold II
3. square de Meeûs
4. place du Luxembourg
5. Le Pullman
6. Noé
7. Musée de l'Institute Royal des Sciences Naturelles
8. Musée Wiertz
9. European Parliament Buildings
10. Parc Léopold
11. Maison Antoine
12. Council of the European Communities
13. Info Point Europe
14. Berlaymont Building
15. Bodeguilla
16. Maison Saint-Cyr
17. Maison Van Eetvelde
18. Maison Deprez-Van de Velde
19. square Marie-Louise
20. The Wild Geese
21. Kitty O'Shea's
22. Parc du Cinquantaire
23. Pavillon Horta
24. Musée Royal de l'Armée et d'Histoire Militaire
25. Autoworld
26. Musées Royaux d'Art et d'Histoire
27. Atelier de Moulages
28. Maison de Paul Cauchie
Continue tour,
look at map 1 (p.35):
29. Cristallerie Anspach
30. Brüsel
31. Au Suisse
32. 100% Design
33. Virgin Megastore

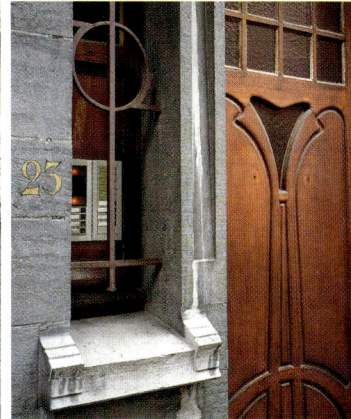

Ixelles and St. Gilles

Art Nouveau rose to popularity at the end of the 19th century and swept through European cities like Paris, Berlin and Brussels assuming the additional names of 'Jugendstil' (youth style) and Liberty Style. The aesthetic is defined by its use of flowing lines, organic shapes and floral motifs. Brussels' Victor Horta was, undoubtedly, one of the style's masters. Other 'belle époque' designers also thrived within the city, including Paul Hankar, Gustave Strauven and Paul Cauchie. Art Nouveau first appeared in Brussels in 1893 with Victor Horta's Hôtel Tassel, and the style blossomed as the city's population rose and inhabitants began constructing homes within and around city limits.

Legend

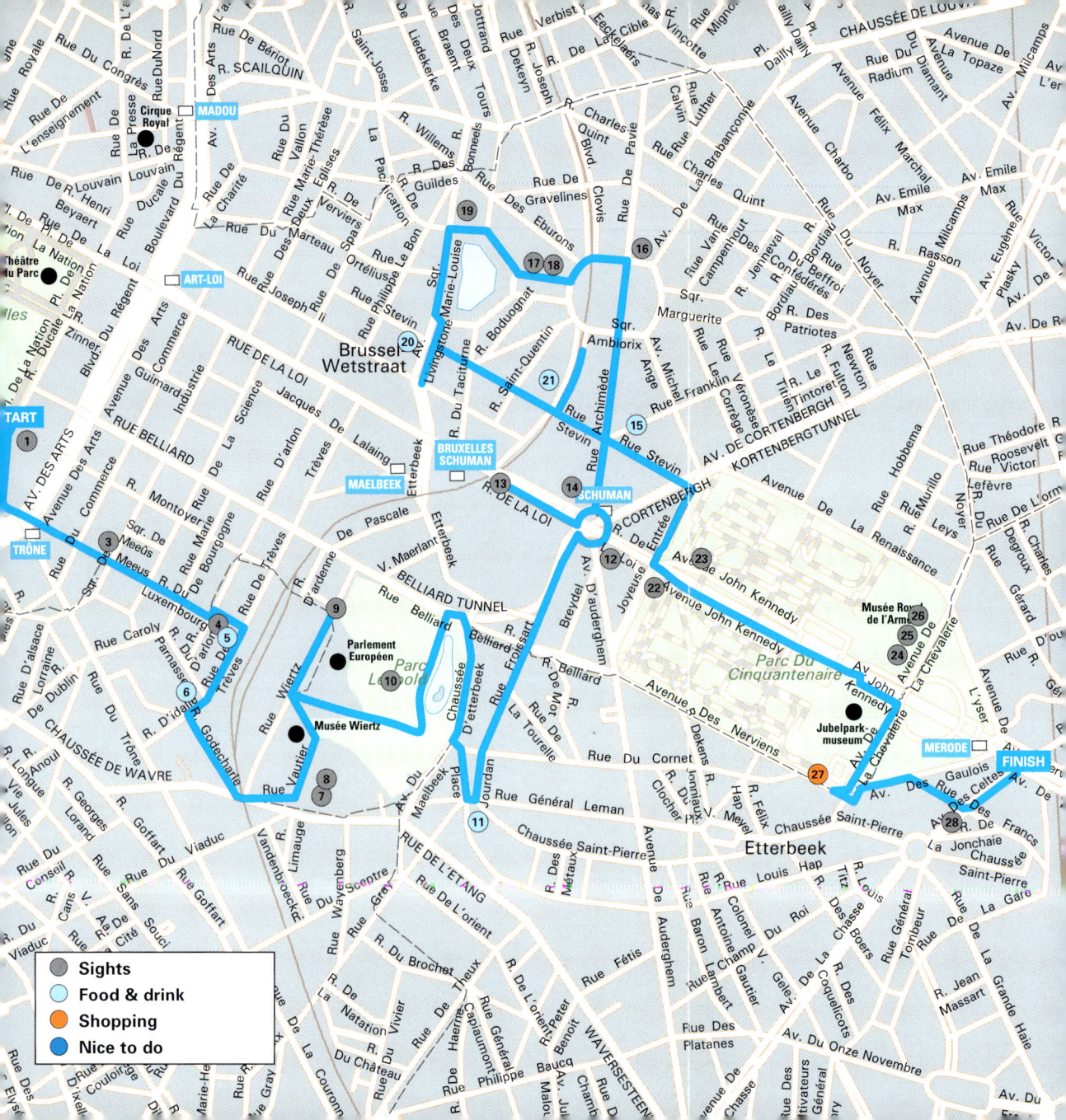

- ● Sights
- ○ Food & drink
- ● Shopping
- ● Nice to do

MADOU · ART-LOI · TRÔNE · MAELBEEK · BRUXELLES SCHUMAN · SCHUMAN · MERODE

Cirque Royal
Théâtre du Parc
Brussel Wetstraat
Parlement Européen
Parc Léopold
Musée Wiertz
Musée Royal de l'Armée
Jubelpark-museum
Parc Du Cinquantenaire
Etterbeek

FINISH

RUE DE LA LOI · RUE BELLIARD · BELLIARD TUNNEL · CHAUSSÉE DE WAVRE · AV. DE CORTENBERGH · KORTENBERGTUNNEL · Avenue John Kennedy · RUE DE L'ÉTANG

Sights

(1) **Hôtel Solvay** was designed by Victor Horta for Ernest Solvay (1838-1922), a chemist who discovered a process for creating soda, named the Solvay process. Solvay went on to become a great Belgian industrialist and humanitarian. The exterior of this home is praised for its elegant metalwork and use of colorful stones. It contains its original furnishings and fittings in marble, teak and mahogany.
224 avenue louise, not open for public, metro louise

(2) **Hôtel Tassel** is the celebrated 'first house' of Victor Horta and is generally recognized as the first building in the world for which the techniques of Art Nouveau were applied to architecture. As Horta's first commission, for industrialist Emile Tassel, this home put Horta and Art Nouveau in Brussels on the map. Horta is known for his restrained façades, but this one is a bit more flamboyant. Note the spiraling ironwork and the magnificent stained glass. Although you can't visit inside, the interior is the real masterpiece - a glass dome adds to the interior light. You'll just have to imagine it.
6 rue paul-emile janson, not open for public, metro louise

(3) **No. 48 rue Defacqz**, Paul Hankar built Maison Camberlani in 1897 for the Italian Symbolist painter Albert Ciamberlani. With one of the finest Art Nouveau exteriors in the city, it is adorned with huge round windows on the first floor and a sgraffiti frieze representing the Ages of Man.
48 rue defacqz, not open for public, metro louise

(4) **No. 50 rue Defacqz** was built by Hankar in 1898 for the painter René Janssens. Though it was drastically altered in 1905, you can still note the extravagant brickwork and ornate window treatments.
50 rue detacqz, not open for public, metro louise

⑤ **No. 71 rue Defacqz**, Maison Hankar was the home of Art Nouveau architect Paul Hankar. A contemporary of Victor Horta, Hankar was a big fan of sgraffiti and multicolored brickwork. His home, which reflects a strong Japanese influence, was also built in 1893, the same year in which Horta created Hôtel Tassel.
71 rue defacqz, not open for public, metro louise

⑥ The **Eglise de la Trinité** (Trinity Church) is admittedly a bit run down, however it still remains a formidable baroque structure in the midst of the surrounding square. Its façade was once part of another church that was destroyed to make space for place de Brouckère, and was brought block by block to be reconstructed onto this edifice. There are plans to restore the church, but for now, it remains closed.
parvis de la trinité, metro louise

⑦ **No. 92 rue Africaine** was designed by B. De Lestre in 1903. Note the circular windows and geometric details dominating the façade of this charming cream-colored house. This is a characteristic feature of Art Nouveau architecture.
92 rue africaine, not open for public, metro louise

⑨ **Musée Horta** was Victor Horta's home and studio, built by Horta from 1899 to 1901. It was opened as a museum in 1969 after being purchased by the Commune de Saint-Gilles several years earlier. Its interior is a wonderful study of Horta's style, with an elegant spiral staircase, a magnificent terrace and a stunning winter garden. Even the smallest details, a flowing coat hook and hat stand, reflect his masterful touch. Pay attention to Horta's manipulation of light, exemplified by his glass canopy above the stairwell.
23-25 rue américaine, telephone 025 37 16 92, open tue-sun 2pm-5.30pm, admission €5, metro louise

⑩ **Nos. 53 and 55 avenue Brugmann** were both built by Edouard Pelseneer in 1898 and 1899 respectively. Number 55, called Les Hiboux (the owls), has two false chimneys, on top of which are perched two owls.
53 and 55 avenue brugmann not open for public, metro louise

RUE DEFACQZ 50 ④

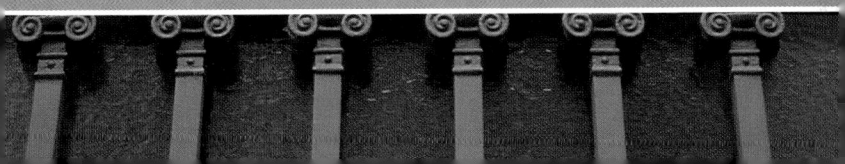

⑪ **Hôtel Hannon** now serves as a gallery for temporary photography exhibitions, renamed **L'Espace Photographique Contretype**. It is the only Art Nouveau house, aside from the Horta Museum, that you can visit on a daily basis. Built in 1903 by Jules Brunfaut for the industrialist Edouard Hannon, (who incidentally was a figurehead in the Solvay soda empire), the house features a stunning stairwell adorned with an enormous fresco and windows equipped with Tiffany glass. Emile Gallé was originally commissioned to design all the furnishings and other accessories, but the house was abandoned for many years and most of these furnishings were sold. Edouard Hannon was also an amateur photographer who helped pioneer landscape photography. His photos are displayed alongside other photographic pieces.
1 avenue de la jonction, telephone 025 38 42 20, open tue-sun 1pm-6pm, admission €2.50, metro louise

⑫ **Nos. 74 and 79 Rue de la Réforme** utilize elements attributed to Art Nouveau architecture. Note the murals on no. 79 and the intricate ironworks and murals on no. 74.
74 and 79 rue de la réforme, not open for public, metro louise

⑬ **Musée Constantin Meunier** was once the home of the Belgian painter and sculptor by the same name, who produced over 800 works within his lifetime. The museum contains more than 300 of his pieces, which feature industrial and farm workers, a kind of social realism.
59 rue de l'abbaye, telephone 026 48 44 49, opening tue-sun 10am-noon, 1pm-5pm, closed alternate weekends, admission free, metro louise

⑭ **Bois de la Cambre** is an idyllic wooded area in the midst of the city that used to be part of the Soignes Forest. Enjoy a cup of tea at one of the tearooms along the lake and later attend a performance at the avant-garde Théâtre de Poche inside its confines. You really have to venture deep inside the 50 acres of trees and greenery to get away from the sounds of traffic.
intersection of avenue louise and boulevard de la cambre, metro louise

(15) **Nos. 46, 44 and 42 rue de Bellevue** were designed by the prolific Art Nouveau architect Antoine Blérot, who created over 200 houses in just eight years. Unfortunately, only 50 of these have survived. Notice the curving stonework and murals, both characteristic of his work.
46, 44 and 42 rue de bellevue, not open for public, metro louise

(16) **Nos. 32 and 30 rue de Bellevue** were also created by Blérot and reflect his attempts to place emphasis on light and space.
32 and 30 rue de bellevue, not open for public, metro louise

(17) **No. 30 rue du Monastère** is another by Blérot and is thought to be his first commissioned house. Dating from 1897, the building is rather restrained, with the exception of the obvious Art Nouveau ironwork.
30 rue du monastère, not open for public, metro louise

(18) **Abbaye de la Cambre** was founded during the 12th century by a woman named Gisèle who was part of the Citeaux Order. The abbey was destroyed during the Wars of Religion in the 16th century. It was later rebuilt and destroyed several times, until 1796 when the order was completely dissolved. A charming French garden (laid out in the 1720s) surrounds the complex, which now houses the National Geographical Institute, the Institute of Decorative Arts and Architecture, and an art exhibition center.
11 avenue emile duray, telephone 026 48 11 21, open mon-fri 9am-noon & 3pm-6pm, sat 3pm-6pm, sun 8am-12.30pm & 3pm-6pm, catholic feast days 9am-noon, admission free, metro louise

(19) The **Abbey Church** in the Abbaye de la Cambre is a 14th century Gothic church, the only building in the abbey to have survived over the centuries. The vaulted ceiling in the nave is lined with wood, and modern stained glass embellishes the semicircular apse.
11 avenue emile duray, telephone 026 48 11 21, open mon-fri 9am-noon & 3pm-6pm, sat 3pm-6pm, sun 8am-12.30pm & 3pm-6pm, catholic feast days 9am-noon, admission free, metro louise

20 **Etangs d'Ixelles** (the ponds of Ixelles) are recommended to visit during the warmer months when they are filled with ducks, and fishermen are scattered about the edges. There used to be several ponds that lined the River Maelbeek, but these are the only survivors.
avenue général charles de gaulle, open daily 24 hours, admission free, metro louise

21 **Nos. 38 and 39 avenue Général Charles de Gaulle** were designed by Antoine Blérot and overlook the Etangs d'Ixelles. Attractive iron banisters lead up to both front doors. At one point, Blérot's own home stood between these two, but it was destroyed by fire in the 1960s.
38 and 39 avenue général charles de gaulle, metro porte de namur or louise

22 The **Musée Communal d'Ixelles** was founded in 1892 and is a small, informal gallery hosting fantastic modern art exhibits. Works by Belgian artists such as Magritte, Rik Wouters and Delvaux are in the permanent collection, as well as a selection of posters by French artist Toulouse-Lautrec. Picasso's Guitar and Fruit Bowl is one of the museum's many highlights.
71 rue j. van volsem, telephone 025 15 64 21, open tue-fri 1pm-7pm, sat-sun 10am-5pm, admission free for permanent collection, metro porte de namur

Food & drink

(8) **La Quincaillerie** was once an ironmonger's shop, and today it's one of the trendiest restaurants in Brussels. The décor refers to its days as an iron shop - hundreds of drawers, a giant wall clock, and a myriad of levels on which to dine. This bistro has been patronized by a variety of European celebrities, including Helmut Kohl and Gérard Depardieu. Dishes include game, meat and seafood, which is the house specialty.
45 rue du page, telephone 025 38 25 53, open mon-fri noon-2.30pm, 7pm-midnight, sat-sun & holidays 7pm-midnight, price €37, metro louise

(24) **Dolma** is a vegetarian's dream in a city that mostly dines on meat and fish. A variety of delicious meat-free delights line the sumptuous buffet. Aside from tofu and quorn dishes, quiches and tarts are also available. There's also a health food store next to the restaurant.
329 chaussée d'ixelles, telephone 026 49 89 91, open mon-sat noon-2pm & 7pm-10pm, price €12 for buffet, metro porte de namur

(25) **L'Amour Fou** is characterized by great ambiance and great food. This is one of the few cafés in the country where the smoking section is actually separated from the non-smoking section. Apart from that convenience, the bistro-style menu (salads, pastas and steaks) offers up a wide selection of delicious dishes. The dame blanche (hot fudge sundae) is a must-have on a warm afternoon.
185 chaussée d'ixelles, telephone 023 51 43 94, open daily 9am-midnight, price €8, metro porte de namur

(26) **Yamayu Santatsu** is a jewel of a Japanese restaurant. First of all, it's filled with Japenese diners - always a good sign. There's a sushi chef at the counter, and the sushi and the sashimi are excellent. But there's more to this place than just raw fish. The menu also boasts tempura, nabe (beef, tofu and vegetables in a casserole served steaming at your table) and sake. Book in advance and enjoy.
141 chaussée d'ixelles, telephone 025 13 53 12, open tue-sat noon-2pm & 7pm-10pm, sun 7pm-10pm, price €50, metro porte de namur

SOUNDS

(27) **Sounds** has been the venue of choice for many celebrated international and local jazz musicians for the past 20 years, yet it's still a gem undiscovered by the masses. Saturdays play host to the bigger names in jazz, but the entrance fee is still quite affordable. During the week, entrance is free.
28 rue de la tulipe, telephone 025 12 92 50, open mon-sat noon-midnight, admission between €5 and €7.50 weekends, metro porte de namur

(31) **Le Tournant** is a restaurant and wine shop run by Congo-born Belgian Michel Dehoux, who weaves together a variety of tastes and textures from Africa, the Antilles and South America. Such European 'norms' as foie gras and cheese with apple purée are also on the menu. Try the lamb with courgette seeds from Ghana, followed by an apricot tart with green pepper for dessert. Daring and delicious.
168 chaussée de wavre, telephone 025 02 61 65, open tue-thu 6pm-midnight, fri-sat 6pm-1am, price €10, metro porte de namur

Shopping

(23) **Chaussée d'Ixelles** is filled with affordable options in the form of shops like H&M and Mango. There are also several small indoor malls situated near the end of the avenue close to the entrance of the Porte de Namur metro.
chaussée d'ixelles, metro porte de namur

(28) **Look 50** has a nice selection of second-hand clothes, if you are willing to invest the time it takes to sift through the racks. The shop is best known for its vintage Levi's.
10 rue de la paix, telephone 025 12 24 18, open mon-sat 10am-6.30pm, metro porte de namur

(30) **African Asian Foods** is quite a treat, if only for the people watching and the exotic selection of foods. This shop is located in the heart of one of Brussels' immigrant districts (the area, dubbed Matongé, is predominately inhabited by Central Africans). If you hunger for salted fish and plantains, you're in luck!
25 chaussée de wavre, no telephone, open mon-sat 9am-8pm, metro porte de namur

Nice to do

(29) **Vendôme** is a five-screen cinema, showing a large selection of arthouse films as well as a smattering of some more mainstream fare. At least two screens feature English language films at any given time.
18 chaussée de wavre, telephone 025 02 37 00, admission €7, metro porte de namur

Ixelles and St. Gilles

Begin at Hôtel Solvay ①. Just off avenue Louise, walk down Bailli and turn right on rue de Livourne. Turn right again on rue Paul-Emile Janson ②. Retrace your steps on P.E. Janson until you reach rue Faider. Turn right and right again on rue Defacqz ③ ④. Retrace your steps and continue along Defacqz ⑤. Turn left down rue de l'Amazone to the Eglise de la Trinité church ⑥. Continue to rue de l'Aqueduc and turn right. Turn left on rue Africaine ⑦ and turn left again on chaussée de Waterloo. Continue until you reach rue du Page and turn left ⑧. Retracing steps on rue du Page, turn right on rue Americain. The Musée Horta ⑨ will be on your left. Make a left on chaussée de Charleroi (turns into avenue Brugmann ⑩), until you reach avenue de la Jonction ⑪. Across avenue Brugmann, find avenue du Haute-Pont. Turn left on rue Franz Merjay, and then make the first right on rue de la Réforme ⑫. Continue until you reach avenue Louis Lepoutre, where you should turn left, and then make a right on chaussée de Waterloo. Eventually, you will veer left on rue de l'Abbaye ⑬ and continue down until you reach avenue Louise. A right onto Louise leads to the entrance of the Bois de la Cambre ⑭, or continue instead onto rue de Bellevue ⑮ ⑯. Make another right on rue du Monestère ⑰ and follow it to the entrance of the Abbaye de la Cambre ⑱ ⑲. Exit the abbey via Monestère. Take the first right, then the first left into a lane that borders a park to your right. This road will become avenue Général Charles de Gaulle, and it runs along-side the Etangs d'Ixelles ⑳ ㉑. Walk until you reach place Eugène Flagey and go onto rue Malibran. Make a left onto rue du Collège. Turn right on rue Jean van Volsem ㉒. Backtrack on Volsem to reach chaussée d'Ixelles ㉓ ㉔ ㉕ ㉖ and turn right. Feel free to take a jazz detour ㉗, or a shopping detour ㉘. Near the bottom of the chaussée, turn right on chaussée de Wavré to discover the Matongé district ㉙ ㉚ ㉛.

6 Musts!

Parc de Laeken

Explore this magnificent spot of greenery just outside Brussels.

Serres Royales de Laeken

If possible, visit the Serres Royales de Laeken.

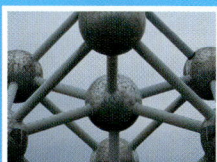

Atomium

Go to the top, and enjoy the view from the Atomium.

Bruparck

Have dinner in Bruparck Village, a replica of an traditional Belgian village.

Mini Europe

Visit a miniature version of Europe at Mini Europe.

Antiek Blaes

Come to Antiek Blaes to purchase the coolest gifts.

● Sights
● Shopping
○ Food & drink
● Nice to do

6

and Mini-Europe, for those who desire to see as much of Europe as possible in the shortest amount of time. Afterwards, one can metro into Porte de Hal and explore one of the shopping gems of Brussels, rue Blaes in the Marolles district. This entire street is filled with wonderful antique and second-hand shops. Then round the evening out with a bit of clubbing until dawn.

1. Hôtel Solvay
2. Hôtel Tassel
3. No. 48 Rue Defacqz
4. No. 50 Rue Defacqz
5. No. 71 Rue Defacqz
6. Eglise de la Trinité
7. No. 5 Rue Africaine
8. La Quincaillerie
9. Musée Horta
10. Nos. 53 & 55 Avenue Brugmann
11. Hôtel Hannon (L'Espace Photographique Contretype)
12. Nos. 74 & 79 Rue de la Réforme
13. Musée Constantin Meunier
14. Bois de la Cambre
15. Nos. 46, 44 & 42 Rue de Bellevue
16. Nos. 32 & 30 Rue de Bellevue
17. No. 30 Rue du Monastère
18. Abbaye de la Cambre
19. Abbey Church
20. Etangs d'Ixelles
21. Nos. 38 & 39 Avenue Général de Gaulle
22. Musée Communal d'Ixelles
23. Chaussée d'Ixelles
24. Dolma
25. L'Amour Fou
26. Yamayu Santatsu
27. Sounds
28. Look 50
29. Vendôme
30. African Asian Foods
31. Le Tournant

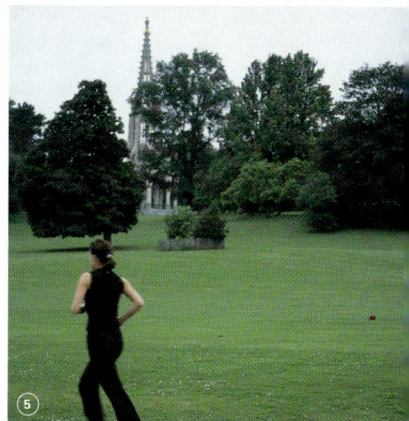

- ● Sights
- ◯ Food & drink
- ● Shopping
- ● Nice to do

Laeken and rue Blaes

The official royal palace may be in the center of Brussels, but the royal family chooses to spend most of its time amidst the lush parks of Laeken. Discover the legacy of Léopold II in the form of the Chinese Pavilion and Japanese Tower, and cast your eyes upon the beautiful greenhouses situated on the royal grounds. The bordering neighborhood of Heysel is graced by what many consider to be an eyesore (though it was once thought to be a great achievement), the Atomium. Created for the 1958 World's Fair in Brussels, it is, in function, the equivalent of Paris' Eiffel Tower - though not as celebrated. This tour is a delight for young and old as it leads to wonderfully kitschy locales such as Bruparck - a low-maintenance amusement park,

Sights

(1) **Notre-Dame de Laeken** was built in memory of Belgium's first Queen, Louise Marie, by renowned Belgian architect Joseph Poelaert (who built the Palais de Justice). This place of worship, erected in neo-Gothic style, has essentially become the royal church.
parvis notre dame, telephone 025 13 89 40, open sun 2pm-5pm, metro bockstael

(2) **The Royal Crypt**, located under Notre-Dame de Laeken, is the resting place for many of the country's royals. It holds the remains of Kings Léopold I, II and III, Albert I and Baudouin I, as well as Queen Astrid, wife of Léopold III, and Princess Charlotte, daughter of Léopold I.
parvis notre dame, telephone 025 13 89 40, open apr-oct first sun of month 3pm-5pm and on anniversary of deaths of kings and queen astrid, admission free, metro bockstael

(3) **Cimetière de Laeken** is the final resting placing for many of Belgium's notables, including architects Joseph Poelaert and Alphonse Balat, and artist Jef Dillen, whose tomb is easily distinguished by its copy of Rodin's The Thinker which adorns it. Most of the tombs located near the entrance date back to the 19th century.
avenue du parc royal, telephone 025 13 89 40, open daily 8.30am-4.30pm, closed sep 20 and nov 15, admission free, metro bockstael

(4) The **Queen Astrid Monument** is best described as a 'temple' created in memory of Swedish Princess Astrid who was married to King Léopold III. Much loved by Belgians, she died in a tragic car accident in Switzerland in 1935 at the tender age of 29. She left behind three children: Joséphine-Charlotte who married the Grand-Duke of Luxemburg; Baudouin I who was Belgian king from 1951-1993; and the current King Albert II.
avenue du parc royal, metro bockstael

(5) **Parc de Laeken** is a leafy oasis located across from the Château Royal.
In it rests Villa Belvédère, the home of King Albert II and Queen Paola; and
the Stuyvenbergh Castle, which was once the home of Emperor Charles V's
architect Louis Van Bodeghem. Today, it is the residence of Fabiola, the
widow of Albert II's predecessor, King Baudouin. Unfortunately, and for
obvious reasons, these chateaux cannot be visited.
avenue du parc royal, open daily 24 hour, admission free, metro bockstael

(6) The **Léopold I Monument** is a neo-Gothic structure created in 1881 to
honor King Léopold I, who reigned from 1831-1865. Léopold was the first
king of Belgium and was a Protestant in this intensely Catholic country. So
controversial was his religious persuasion that, when he died, Cardinal
Sterckx refused to allow his funeral inside Notre-Dame de Laeken. Instead,
a crude memorial structure was erected outside the church before the body
was transferred to the church's basement - now deemed the Royal Crypt.
place de la dynastie, metro bockstael

(7) **Château Royal de Laeken** is the main home of Crown Prince Philippe
and his wife Princess Mathilde. The château was built in 1790 and boasts
Napoleon, who stayed here on several occasions, as a famous occupant.
In fact, it was here that Napoleon signed the declaration of war on Russia
in 1812. Parts of the château were destroyed in a fire in 1890, but a large
part of that has been restored.
avenue du parc royal, metro bockstael

(8) The **Serres Royales de Laeken** are a number of large greenhouses
(the largest rises to 82 ft [25 m]) occupying the royal grounds. Built for
Léopold II by Alphonse Balat (who instructed Victor Horta), they cover four
acres and contain an almost infinite variety of Mediterranean and tropical
plants and flowers. Here's a fair warning - these structures are only open
for ten days a year and the lines are tremendous!
*61 avenue du parc royal (domaine royal), telephone 025 13 89 40, open for
guided tours end apr-early may mon-tue 9am-4pm, fri 8am-11am, sat-sun
9.30am-4pm, admission €2, metro bockstael*

⑩ **PAVILLON CHINOIS**

⑨ The **Neptune Fountain** is a copy of the 16th century original (1563-1566) created by Giovanni Bologna and found in the Piazza del Nettuno in Bologna, Italy. Born in Flanders as Jean Boulogne, Giovanni Bologna was a master of small bronzes. The decorative fountain erected in Bologna is the sculptor's first major work. It's subject, the god Neptune (known in Greek as Poseidon), is depicted in a commanding pose, as if frozen mid-stride. Water flows from the breasts of mermaids rising from the basin at the corners.
intersection of avenue du parc royal and avenue van praet, metro heysel

⑩ **Pavillon Chinois** was built, on the orders of Léopold II, to replicate a Chinese pavilion after he had come across one at the 1900 World's Fair in Paris. Designed by oriental architecture specialist Alexandre Marcel (1860-1928), this pavilion is home to a wonderful collection of Chinese and Japanese porcelain.
44 avenue van praet, telephone 022 68 16 08, open tue-sun 10am-4.45pm, admission €3, metro heysel

⑪ The **Tour Japonaise** is a copy of a 17th century Buddhist pagoda and was also constructed by Marcel at the request of Léopold II. The entrance halls, however, were designed and built in Japan and were shipped over. Today only the lower level can be visited, and it serves as a venue for various temporary exhibitions displaying artifacts from the Far East.
44 avenue van praet, telephone 022 68 16 08, open tue-sun 10am-4.45pm, admission €2.25, metro heysel

Food & drink

㉓ **Chez Richard** caters to a buzzing crowd all day - from suit-and-tied office workers to trendy club kids at night. This bar/café near the Sablon serves up both delicious snacks as well as tasty drinks, and at night, space is cleared to create a little dance floor.

2 rue des minimes, telephone 025 12 14 06, open mon-wed 7am-2am, thu-sat 7am-3am, sun 9am-9pm, price €10, metro louise

Shopping

(17) **Rue Blaes** is a terrific shopping street for those interested in antiques and second-hand bargains. There are stores here catering to every interest, whether it's nautical paraphernalia, at La Fiancée du Pirate at no. 118 or vintage clothing at Idiz Bogam at no. 162.
rue blaes, metro porte de hal

(19) **Modes** is a fantastic vintage clothing shop! It's got everything - Panama hats, straw hats, jewelry, belts, sandals… you name it.
164 rue blaes, telephone 025 03 54 00, open tue-fri 10am-2.30pm, sat-sun 10am-3.30pm, metro porte de hal

(20) **Patricia Shop** is filled with underwear. If La Perla is just too expensive, this is a great alternative for some terrific bargains. Rustle through the bins for good deals on quality pieces.
158 rue blaes, telephone 025 13 36 48, open tue-sat 9.30am-6pm, sun 9.30am-noon, metro porte de hal

㉑ **Bali-Africa** is filled wall-to-wall with African and Asian items, including bongos, statues, masks and furnishings. There are several rooms through which to weave your way, as this shop has over 1,200 square yards of artifacts originating from the Far East, Africa and South America.
154-156 rue blaes, telephone 025 14 47 92, open tue-sat 9am-6pm, sun 9am-4pm, metro porte de hal

㉒ **Antiek Blaes** sells wonderful second-hand items like antique leather footballs, 1950s grooming sets, magnifying glasses, old letter openers, and even boxing gloves. If you've got someone who needs an extra special gift, this shop is your best bet.
51 rue blaes, telephone 025 12 12 99, open mon-sat 10am-6pm, sun 10am-4pm, metro porte de hal or louise

Nice to do

⑫ The **Atomium**, designed by engineer André Waterkeyn, was created for the 1958 World's Fair in Brussels. The image is of an iron atom enlarged 165 billion times. Its nine enormous spheres represent Belgium's nine provinces (although there are now ten) and are held together by iron corridors. You can take an elevator to the top for a view of the entire city. There is also an unremarkable science exhibition located in one of the spheres.
boulevard du centenaire, telephone 024 74 89 77, open sep-mar 10am-6pm, apr-aug 9am-8pm, admission €4.95, metro heysel

⑬ During the World's Fair, a favorite attraction was called 'Merry Belgium'. This feature was an amalgamation of traditional Belgian bars meant to illustrate the country's high quality of living. Today, the attraction has been renamed **Bruparck**, and it can be visited year-round. The bars and restaurants in the Village have pleasing terraces, and there is a playground, a Cyber Café and a gorgeous Venetian Carousel.
20 boulevard du centenaire, telephone 024 78 05 50, open apr-jun 9.30am-6pm, 1-19 jul, 20-31 aug 9.30am-8pm, 20 jul-19 aug 9.30am-midnight, 1 sep-6 jan 10am-6pm, 6 jan-31 mar closed, park admission free, admission to attractions additional, metro heysel

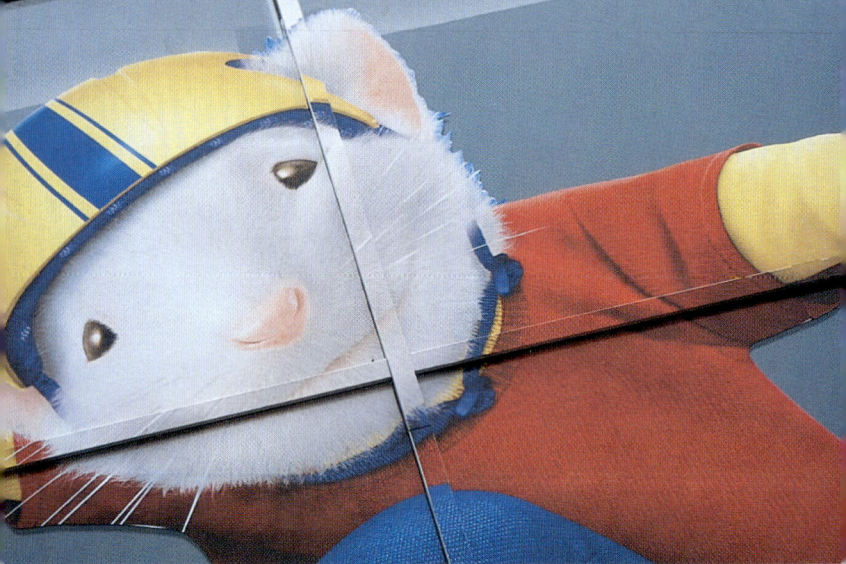

(14) The **Kinepolis** is a 27-screen cinema complex inside Bruparck, where one can take in a number of mainstream releases or an Imax film. This place is absolutely overflowing with children!
1 boulevard du centenaire, bruparck, telephone 024 74 26 00, metro heysel

(15) **Océade** is the popular water-park located inside Bruparck. It includes a wide range of attractions, such as high-speed slides, wavepools, saunas and whirlpools.
20 boulevard du centenaire, bruparck, telephone 024 78 43 20, open school holidays wed-fri 10am-6pm, sat-tue 10am-10pm, admission €12.15 (for 4 hours), metro heysel

(16) **Mini Europe** is a reconstruction of all the highlights of Europe on two hectares of land. All European attractions are reduced to 1/25th of their actual size, except for the Eiffel Tower, which is much smaller in scale. The press of a button makes Mount Vesuvius erupt. You can tear down the Berlin Wall. Miniature trees and plants in the park make everything seem realistic in scale.
20 boulevard du centenaire, bruparck, telephone 024 74 13 11, open apr-jun 9.30am-6pm, jul-aug 9.30am-midnight, oct-mar 10am-6pm, admission €11, metro heysel

(18) **Fuse** is a popular weekly techno, jungle and house party, showcasing some of Europe's most popular DJs. The three-tiered nightclub also hosts Démence and D-Light for the gay and lesbian crowd. Démence (for men) is the last Sunday of each month, while D-Light (for women) takes place on the last Friday of each month.

208 rue blaes, telephone 025 11 97 89, open fri-sat 10pm-7am, admission before 11pm €2.50, after 11pm €10, metro porte de hal

Laeken and rue Blaes

From the Bockstael metro station, turn left at rue Léopold I and follow it to parvis Notre-Dame where you'll find Notre-Dame de Laeken ① ②. Walk around the west side of the church, until the entrance to the Cimetière de Laeken ③. Continue to the opposite side of avenue du Parc Royal. Turn left and continue just past rue des Vignes. On your right, is a park ④. Continue up avenue du Parc Royal. At the first park gate, cross back over the avenue and follow the gravel path flanked by the avenue (right) and the Caserne Sainte-Anne barracks (left). Once you reach the fountain, you've come to the entrance of the Parc de Laeken ⑤. Turn left on the avenue des Trembles and make the first right on avenue des Narcisses (signage is poor here) until place de la Dynastie ⑥. From here, you have a view down to the royal residence ⑦. Walk down avenue de la Dynastie and around the fence to the right of the gates. Continue up avenue du Parc Royal and you'll see the Tour Japonais. In the foreground are the tops of the Serres Royales du Laeken ⑧. Continue up the avenue until a junction ⑨. Turn right on avenue Jan van Praet, with the Pavillon Chinois ⑩ and the Tour Japonaise ⑪. You can travel from one structure to the other via an underground tunnel. Double back to the Neptune Fountain and walk straight ahead on avenue de Madrid. Turn left on to a path that runs along the left-hand side of the modern circular building. This path will lead you to avenue du Gros Tilleul. Half-circle the roundabout and continue on Tilleul until place L. Steens. Just over a third of the way around the square is boulevard du Centenaire, and in the midst of it is the Atomium ⑫. Follow the signs to Bruparck ⑬ ⑭ ⑮ ⑯, which lies about 219 yards (200m) to the northeast. Not far from Bruparck you'll find the Heysel metro stop. Board there and take the metro to Porte de Hal. From here, follow rue du Remblai just off to the left from the North end-exit of the station (look at map tour 2, page 55). Turn right on rue Blaes ⑰ ⑱ ⑲ ⑳ ㉑ ㉒. Head to Chez Richard ㉓ by turning right off rue Blaes on to rue Porte-Rouge and left on rue des Minimes.

ROI AUDOUIN
Av. De Lima
R. Du Disque
Rue Du Disque
FINISH
HEYSEL
14-16
Rampe Des Hollandais
Av. Des Athlètes
Avenue Impératrice Charlotte
Charlotte
Boulevard Du Centenaire

Parc D'osseghem
Avenue De L'atomium
Avenue Du Hallier
Av. Du Hallier
Av. Du Hallier
La Passerelle
Av. De

Avenue De Meysse
Avenue De La Croix Rouge
La Brise Busleyden Busleyd
Avenue Mutsaard
Av. Des Pagodes
R. Des Pagodes
Av. Des Pagodes
AVENUE DES

Parc De Forum
De Wand
Avenue De W Wanneco
Gustave

Av. De Marathon
R. De Javelot
Av. Du Football
Du Marathon
Av. De Marathon
Du Championnat
Avenue Du Football
Atomium 12-13
Bouchout
Blvd. Du Centenaire
Avenue Du Gros Tilleul
Avenue Du Gros Tilleul
Avenue Du Gros Tilleul
Avenue Du Gros Tilleul

Av. Des Seringas
Av. Des Tagètes
Avenue Des Trembles

10
9
Av. Praet
11

Jean Palfyn
Av. Houba
R. De Stroper
Av. Emile
hengem
Stiénon
Avenue Jean
Av. Laënnec
Jean-Baptiste Depaire
Av. Adrien Bavet
Av. Edouard Kufferath
Av. Rommelaere
HOUBA BRUGMAN
Rue Du Heysel
Rue Reper Vreven
Rue Du Heysel
R. Félix Sterckx
Av. Houba De Strooper

Parc De Laeken
6
Av. Des Tagètes
Av. De La Dynastie
La Dynastie
Avenue Du Parc Royal
8
7 Château Royal

R. Ernest Masson
Av. Théophile De Baisieux
R. Stuyvenbergh
Ernest Salu
R. De Laubespin
Emile Wauters
Avenue Jean Sobieski
R. Du Cloître
Avenue Du Cloître
STUYVENBERG
Avenue Des Ebéniers

Avenue Des Seringas
Avenue Des Seringas
Avenue Des Seringas
Avenue Des Trembles
Av. Des Trembles
Av. Des Robiniers
5

Gustave Gilson
Rue Gustave Gilson
Av. Léopold Peret
R. Pierre Verschelden
De Greef
R. Smet De Naeyer
R. Jean Heymans
Boulevard Emile Bockstael
R. Pierre Strauwen
Rue Duysburgh

Parc De La Jeunesse
oi Baudouin
De Smet De Naeyer
R. Saint-Norbert
Ledeganck
Rue Du Gaz
Rue Charles Ramaekers
Rue Alfred Stevens
Rue Ter
Rue Du Plast
Siphons
R. Des Horticulteurs
Rue De
Drève Sainte-Anne
R. Des Horticulteurs
Rue Du Verdier
Avenue Du Parc Royal

Domaine Royale

Secrétin Blvd.
Démineurs
Essegh
Rue Jules
R. Mode
R. Emile Delva
R. Vliebergh
R. Fineau
Rue Des
Rue Du
BOCKSTAEL
4
Rue Des Vignes
Rue Mellery

Charles Woeste
R. Esse
R. Steyls
Rue Emile Delva
R. Jan Bollen
R. Jan Bollen
R. Léopold I
Rue Léopold I
Vanham
Fransman
Blvd. R. Léopold I
3
Laken
1-2
BOCKSTAEL
START
R. Breesch
R. Stéphan
Médori
Rue

① Notre-Dame de Laeken
② The Royal Crypt
③ Cimetière de Laeken
④ Queen Astrid Monument
⑤ Parc de Laeken
⑥ Léopold I Monument
⑦ Château Royal de Laeken
⑧ Serres Royales de Laeken
⑨ Neptune Fountain
⑩ Pavillon Chinois
⑪ Tour Japonaise
⑫ Atomium
⑬ Bruparck
⑭ Kinepolis
⑮ Océade
⑯ Mini Europa

Continue tour,
look at map 2 (p.55):
⑰ Rue Blaes
⑱ Fuse
⑲ Modes
⑳ Patricia Shop
㉑ Bali-Africa
㉒ Antiek Blaes
㉓ Chez Richard

- ⬤ **Sights**
- ◯ **Food & drink**
- 🟠 **Shopping**
- 🔵 **Nice to do**

Nightlife

Belgians like to party. While most clubs open Thursday-Saturday at around 10pm, the action doesn't really start happening until past midnight and can continue until 5am or 6am!

(M) **Le Bazaar** is a restaurant, bar and club rolled into one. The club is located in an underground cave and is open Friday and Saturday nights. If you like funk and rock, this is the place to be.
63 rue des capucins, telephone 025 11 26 00, admission €7.50 plus a drink, metro louise

(N) As late night discos go, **Who's Who Land** is a favorite in Brussels and one of its most popular events is the foam party. This place is always packed with techno party revelers, and Sunday nights cater to a gay crowd.
17 rue poinçon, telephone 025 12 52 70, fri-sat 11pm-4am, admission €10, metro anneessens

(O) **Forest National** is the largest concert hall in Belgium, capable of holding 8,000 people. Some of pop's greatest legends have graced its stage, including Michel Jackson, B.B. King and Bon Jovi. On any given night you can groove to the sounds of pop, rock, jazz or techno, or if you're lucky, a little bit of each. For tickets call 070 344 111 or, from within Belgium, call 0900 00 991. Access the box office via the web at www.ticketclub.be.
36 avenue du globe, telephone 0900 00 991, tram 18

(P) The **Beursschouwburg** is a fantastic venue near the Bourse, playing host to contemporary theatre productions, dance and musical performances and art exhibitions. Known for engaging a variety of dynamic groups for each performance series, this venue is a hit among locals. In fact, this is the annual gathering spot for the Belgian hip-hop convention (bet you didn't even know they had one!)
22 rue auguste orts, telephone 025 13 82 90, metro bourse

BOURSE

(Q) **Cirque Royal** was once an indoor circus, but now serves as a great location for concerts and other large-scale events. From fashion shows to Chippendales, this place has got something for everyone.
81 rue de l'enseignement, telephone 022 18 20 15, metro madou

(R) **AB Ancienne-Belgique** seats up to 2,000 people with space for an additional 750 in standing room. This is the number one rock venue in Brussels, showcasing international as well as local bands. More unusual music groups have played here as well, including the Cuban group Buena Vista Social Club.
114 blvd anspach, telephone 025 48 24 24, metro bourse

(S) **Halles de Schaerbeek** was built in 1901 and at that time served as the local food market. Renovated in 1985, today it is a popular performance venue, and the building is one of the few remaining examples of industrial architecture left in the city.
22b rue royale ste marie, telephone 022 18 21 07, admission €8.70 - €22.50, tram 92 or 93

MATONGE BRU XELLES

PORTE DE NAMUR! PORTE DE L'AMOUR?

J'AI SILLONNÉ LE MONDE ENTIER ET JAMAIS JE N'AI VU UNE VILLE COMME BRUXELLES ET UN QUARTIER COMME MATONGE D'IXELLES OÙ TOUT LE MONDE SE MÊLE, (PLUS DE 100 NATIONALITÉS DANS CE SEUL QUARTIER) DIFFICILE DE DÉCRIRE EN UN MOT CE QU'EST MATONGE-BRUXELLES OU BRUXELLES ELLE-MÊME. BRUXELLES EZA VILLE MYTHIQUE. BRUSSEL EZA LOLA (PARADIS). BRUSSEL IS EEN MAGISCHE STAD. BRUSSEL IS HET PARADIJS...

CE QUARTIER FAT ENVAHI...!

BON PRIX

Alphabetical index

100% design   92

a

abbaye de la cambre   104
abbey church   104
african asian foods   112
alfa louise   11
amigo hotel   7
amour fou, l'   108
ancienne-belgique   138
antiek blaes   127
antoine dansaert   29
archiduc, l'   25
arenburg-galeries   30
atelier de la truffe noire   46
atelier de moulages   92
atomium   128
au suisse   91
autoworld   87
avenue brugmann nos. 53 & 55 100
avenue de la toison d'or   49
avenue général charles de
gaulle, nos. 38 & 39   106
avenue louise   51

b

bali-africa   127
bazaar, le   136
bedford hotel   11
berlaymont building   83
beursschouwburg   136
bibliothèque royale albert I   61
bodeguilla   88
bois de la cambre   103

bonsoir clara   26
botanique, le   72
boulevard waterloo   49
bourse   22
british war memorial   40
bruparck   128
brüsel   92
buses   14

c

café le perroquet   46
café métropole   26
cartier   51
caserne des pompiers   52
cathédrale des sts michel
et gudule   67
centre belge de la bande
dessinée   33
centre culturel de la
communauté française
wallonie-bruxelles   67
chanel   51
chapelle de nassau   61
chapelle royale   65
château royal de laeken   120
chaussée d'ixelles   112
chez richard   124
cimetière de laeken   119
cirque royal   138
colonne du congres   67
comme chez soi   45
conrad international brussels   8
council of the european
communities   83

cristallerie anspach   92

d

delvaux   29
dixseptième, le   11
dolma   108
dôme, le   12

e

eglise de la trinité   100
eglise de minimes   43
eglise des brigittines   39
eglise notre dame de la
chapelle   39
eglise notre dame du sablon   40
eglise sainte marie   67
eglise saint-jacques-sur-
coudenberg   62
emporio armani   49
espace photographique
contretype, l'   103
etangs d'ixelles   106
european parliament buildings   81

f

forest national   136
fountain of minerve   39
fuse   131

g

galeries st. hubert   29
godfrey de bouillon, statue of   62
grand place   19
grand, le   71
gucci   49

h

halles de schaerbeek   138
hotel de ville   20
hôtel hannon   103
hôtel solvay   99
hôtel tassel   99
hotels   7-12
house of bellevue   65

i

indigo   46
info point europe   83

j

janneken pis   19
jardin botanique   67
jardin d'egmont   40
java, le   25

k

kartchma, la   45
kasbah   26
kinepolis   131
kitty o'shea's   91

l

léopold I monument   120
librarie histoire   71
look 50   112

m

maison antoine   88
maison de paul cauchie   87
maison deprez-van de velde   84
maison saint-cyr   83
maison van eetvelde   84
manneken pis   21

mary chocolatier 71

meridien, le 8

metro 14

métropole 7

mini europe 131

modes 125

mokafé 25

mont des arts 61

musée communal d'ixelles 106

musée constantin meunier 103

musée d'art ancien 62

musée d'art moderne 65

musee de l'hopital sainte-pierre 43

musée de l'hotel charlier 67

musée de l'imprimerie 61

musée de l'institute royal des
sciences naturelles 81

musée de la brasserie 20

musée de la dynastie 65

musée de la ville de bruxelles 19

musée de livre 61

musée des instruments
de musique 62

musée des postes et
telecommunications 39

musée du cacao et du chocolat 19

musée du cinéma 66

musée du cinquantenaire 87

musée du folklore 43

musée horta 100

musée royal de l'armée
et d'histoire militaire 87

musée wiertz 81

musées royaux d'art
et d'histoire 87

n

neptune fountain 123

nightlife 136-138

noé 88

notre dame aux riches claires 21

notre dame de bon secours 21

notre dame du finistère 22

notre-dame de laeken 119

o

océade 131

p

pain quotidien, le 45

palais d'egmont 40

palais de justice 43

palais de la nation 66

palais des acadamies 80

palais des beaux arts 66

palais royale 65

parc de bruxelles 66

parc de laeken 120

parc du cinquantaire 84

parc léopold 81

patricia shop 125

pavillon chinois 123

pavillon horta 84

pieter bruegel the elder,
house of 43

place du grand sablon 49

place du jeu de balle and flea
market 52

place du luxembourg 80

place du petit sablon 40

place royale 62

place st. catherine 26

plaza, le 8

pullman, le 88

q
queen astrid monument 119
quincaillerie, la 108

r
radisson sas 8
ralph lauren 51
restaurant musée des
instruments de musique 68
royal crypt 119
rue africaine, no. 92 100
rue blaes 125
rue de bellevue, nos. 32 & 30 104
rue de bellevue, nos. 46, 44
& 42 104
rue de la réforme, nos. 74 & 79 103
rue defacqz, no. 48 99
rue defacqz, no. 50 99
rue defacqz, no. 71 100
rue des bouchers 25
rue du monastère, no. 30 104
rue neuve 30

s
scientastic 22
serres royales de laeken 120
service de chalcographie 65
skieven architek, de 46
sounds 110
square de meeûs 80
square marie-louise 84
st. jean baptiste au béguinage 21
st. nicolas 22
statue evrard t' serclaes 21
statue of léopold II 80
sterling books 30

stijl men/women 29

t
table de merlin, la 68
taxi 15
the wild geese 91
théâtre de la monnaie 30
théâtre de toone 30
théâtre du rideau de bruxelles 72
théâtre royal du parc 72
thierry mugler 51
tour d'angle 39
tour japonaise 123
tournant, le 110
trams 14
transport 14-15

u
ultieme hallucinatie, de 68
ustel, hotel 12

v
vendôme 113
versace 51
verscheuren 52
via della spiga 30
virgin megastore 92

w
welcome, hotel 11
who's who land 136
wittamer 45

y
yamayu santatsu 108

z
zebra bar 25

HELP WANTED
FULL TIME WAITRESS
(FRENCH + ENGLISH)
EXPERIENCED!

Category index

food & drink

amour fou, l'	108
archiduc, l'	25
atelier de la truffe noire	46
au suisse	91
bodeguilla	88
bonsoir clara	26
café le perroquet	46
café métropole	26
chez richard	124
comme chez soi	45
dolma	108
indigo	46
java, le	25
kartchma, la	45
kasbah	26
kitty o'shea's	91
maison antoine	88
mokafé	25
noé	88
pain quotidien, le	45
place st. catherine	26
pullman, le	88
quincaillerie, la	108
restaurant musée des instruments de musique	68
rue des bouchers	25
skieven architek, de	46
sounds	110
table de merlin, la	68
the wild geese	91
tournant, le	110
ultieme hallucinatie, de	68
wittamer	45
yamayu santatsu	108
zebra bar	25

hotels

alfa louise	11
amigo hotel	7
bedford hotel	11
conrad international brussels	8
dixseptième, le	11
dôme, le	12
meridien, le	8
métropole	7
plaza, le	8
radisson sas	8
ustel, hotel	12
welcome, hotel	11

nice to do

arenburg-galeries	30
atomium	128
botanique, le	72
bruparck	128
fuse	131
kinepolis	131
mini europe	131
océade	131
théâtre de la monnaie	30
théâtre de toone	30
théâtre du rideau de bruxelles	72
théâtre royal du parc	72
vendôme	113

nightlife

ancienne-belgique	138
bazaar, le	136
beursschouwburg	136

cirque royal 138
forest national 136
halles de schaerbeek 138
who's who land 136

shopping
100% design 92
african asian foods 112
antiek blaes 127
antoine dansaert 29
atelier de moulages 92
avenue de la toison d'or 49
avenue louise 51
bali-africa 127
boulevard waterloo 49
brüsel 92
cartier 51
caserne des pompiers 52
chanel 51
chaussée d'ixelles 112
cristallerie anspach 92
delvaux 29
emporio armani 49
galeries st. hubert 29
grand, le 71
gucci 49
librarie histoire 71
look 50 112
mary chocolatier 71
modes 125
patricia shop 125
place du grand sablon 49
place du jeu de balle and
flea market 52
ralph lauren 51
rue blaes 125
rue neuve 30

sterling books 30
stijl men/women 29
thierry mugler 51
versace 51
verscheuren 52
via della spiga 30
virgin megastore 92

sights
abbaye de la cambre 104
abbey church 104
autoworld 87
avenue brugmann nos. 53
& 55 100
avenue général charles de
gaulle, nos. 38 & 39 106
berlaymont building 83
bibliothèque royale albert I 61
bois de la cambre 103
bourse 22
british war memorial 40
cathédrale des sts michel
et gudule 67
centre belge de la bande
dessinée 33
centre culturel de la communauté
française wallonie-bruxelles 67
chapelle de nassau 61
chapelle royale 65
château royal de laeken 120
cimetière de laeken 119
colonne du congres 67
council of the european
communities 83
eglise de la trinité 100
eglise de minimes 43
eglise des brigittines 39

eglise notre dame de la chapelle 39
eglise notre dame du sablon 40
eglise sainte marie 67
eglise saint-jacques-sur-coudenberg 62
espace photographique contretype, l' 103
etangs d'ixelles 106
european parliament buildings 81
fountain of minerve 39
godfrey de bouillon, statue of 62
grand place 19
hotel de ville 20
hôtel hannon 103
hôtel solvay 99
hôtel tassel 99
house of bellevue 65
info point europe 83
janneken pis 19
jardin botanique 67
jardin d'egmont 40
léopold I monument 120
maison de paul cauchie 87
maison deprez-van de velde 84
maison saint-cyr 83
maison van eetvelde 84
manneken pis 21
mont des arts 61
musée communal d'ixelles 106
musée constantin meunier 103
musée d'art ancien 62
musée d'art moderne 65
musee de l'hopital sainte-pierre 43
musée de l'hotel charlier 67
musée de l'imprimerie 61
musée de l'institute royal
des sciences naturelles 81
musée de la brasserie 20
musée de la dynastie 65
musée de la ville de bruxelles 19
musée de livre 61
musée des instruments de musique 62
musee des postes et telecommunications 39
musée du cacao et du chocolat 19
musée du cinéma 66
musée du cinquantenaire 87
musée du folklore 43
musée horta 100
musée royal de l'armée et d'histoire militaire 87
musée wiertz 81
musées royaux d'art et d'histoire 87
neptune fountain 123
notre dame aux riches claires 21
notre dame de bon secours 21
notre dame du finistère 22
notre-dame de laeken 119
palais d'egmont 40
palais de justice 43
palais de la nation 66
palais des acadamies 80
palais des beaux arts 66
palais royale 65
parc de bruxelles 66
parc de laeken 120
parc du cinquantaire 84
parc léopold 81
pavillon chinois 123
pavillon horta 84
pieter bruegel the elder,

house of	43
place du luxembourg	80
place du petit sablon	40
place royale	62
queen astrid monument	119
royal crypt	119
rue africaine, no. 92	100
rue de bellevue, nos. 32 & 30	104
rue de bellevue, nos. 46, 44 & 42	104
rue de la réforme, nos. 74 & 79	103
rue defacqz, no. 48	99
rue defacqz, no. 50	99
rue defacqz, no. 71	100
rue du monastère, no. 30	104
scientastic	22
serres royales de laeken	120
service de chalcographie	65
square de meeûs	80
square marie-louise	84
st. jean baptiste au béguinage	21
st. nicolas	22
statue evrard t' serclaes	21
statue of léopold II	80
tour d'angle	39
tour japonaise	123

transport

buses	14
metro	14
taxi	15
trams	14

RUE NEUVE

This guide has been compiled with the utmost care. mo' media bv cannot be held liable in the case of any inaccuracies within the text. Any remarks or comments should be directed to the following address.

mo' media, attn. 100% brussels,
p.o. box 7028, 4800 ga, breda, the netherlands, e-mail info@momedia.nl

author	taunya renson-martin
final editing	zahra sethna
photography	marieke hüsstege
graphic design	www.studio100procent.nl, naarden
cartography	eurocartografie, hendrik-ido-ambacht
project guidance	joyce enthoven & sasja lagendijk, mo' media
printing office	brepols, turnhout (b)

100% brussels	isbn 90 5767 096 8 - nur 510, 511, 512
	© mo' media, breda, the netherlands, april 2003